Illinois Evidence
with Objections

Illinois Evidence with Objections

James P. Carey
Professor of Law
Loyola University Chicago School of Law

Anthony J. Bocchino
Jack E. Feinberg Professor of Litigation
Temple University Law School

David A. Sonenshein
I. Herman Stern Professor of Law
Temple University Law School

National Institute for Trial Advocacy

NITA 1998 Educational Services Committee

Rudolph F. Pierce, Chair
Goulston & Storrs
Boston, Massachusetts

Joseph R. Bankoff
King & Spalding
Atlanta, Georgia

Patricia C. Bobb
Patricia C. Bobb & Associates
Chicago, Illinois

James J. Brosnahan
Morrison & Foerster
San Francisco, California

Kenneth S. Broun
University of North Carolina
Chapel Hill, North Carolina

Hon. Jim R. Carrigan
Retired
Judicial Arbiter Group
Denver, Colorado

Joseph C. Jaudon
Long & Jaudon, P.C.
Denver, Colorado

No part of this work may be reproduced or transmitted in any form or by any means, electronic or mechanical, including photocopying and recording, or by any information storage or retrieval system without the express written permission of the National Institute for Trial Advocacy unless such copying is expressly permitted by federal copyright law. Address inquiries to:

> Reproduction Permission
> National Institute for Trial Advocacy
> 1602 North Ironwood
> South Bend, Indiana 46635
> (800) 225-6482   FAX (219) 282-1263
> www.nita.org   E-mail nita.1@nd.edu

©1998 by the National Institute for Trial Advocacy
Printed in the United States of America. All rights reserved.

Carey, James P., Anthony J. Bocchino, and David A. Sonenshein, *Illinois Evidence with Objections*, (NITA, 1998).

ISBN 1-55681-537-9

Contents

Preface	xi
Ambiguous Questions	1
Argumentative Questions	2
Asked and Answered Questions	3
Assuming Facts Not in Evidence	4
Authentication of Writings, Photographs, and Recordings	6
Authentication of Telephone Conversation and Voices	10

Character Evidence
- Generally 12
- Parties in a Civil Case 14
- Accused or Victim in a Criminal Case 16
- Accused or Victim in a Criminal Case Specific Instances 18
- Other Acts, Crimes, or Wrongs 20
- Prior Sexual Activity of Alleged Victim 22
- Similar Crimes or Acts in Criminal Sexual Assault Cases: Previous Acts Between Defendant and Victim 25
- Similar Crimes or Acts in Criminal Sexual Assault Cases: Previous Acts of Defendant with Others 28

Competence to Testify	31
The Dead Man's Act	33
Compound Questions	36
Compromise/Offers of Compromise	38

Cross-Examination
  Generally 40
  Scope 42
Exhibits
  Demonstrative 44
  Tangible Objects 47
  Writings 44
Expert Opinion 51
Firsthand Knowledge 54
Guilty Pleas 56
Habit and Routine Practice 58
Hearsay
  Generally 60
  Two Persistent, False Concepts in
    Illinois Law 62
  Attacking and Supporting the Credibility
    of a Hearsay Declarant 64
  Non-Hearsay Admissions 66
  Non-Hearsay Prior Statements
    Child Sexual Abuse 69
    Prior Inconsistent Statements in a
      Criminal Case 71
    Prior Statements of a Witness Who
      Refuses to Testify 74
  Hearsay Within Hearsay 76
Hearsay Exception
  Absence of Entry in Business Records 77
  Absence of Public Records or Entry 79
  Excited Utterance 81

Family Records	83
Former Testimony	85
Judgment of Previous Conviction	87
Market Reports and Mortality Tables	89
Birth, Baptismal, and Similar Certificates	91
Public Records and Reports	93
Police Reports	95
Recorded Recollection	98
Records of Regularly Conducted Activity	100
Records of Vital Statistics	105
Reputation as to Character	107
Reputation Concerning Personal or Family History	109
Requirement of Unavailability for Certain Hearsay Exceptions	111
Declaration Against Interest	114
Statements in Ancient Documents	117
Statement of Personal or Family History	119
Statements for Purposes of Medical Diagnosis or Treatment	121
Statements for Purposes of Medical Diagnosis or Treatment in Sexual Abuse Prosecutions	124
Dying Declaration	126
Then-Existing Mental, Emotional, or Physical Condition	128

Impeachment

Bias, Prejudice, Interest, and Improper Motive	130
Character Evidence	133

Learned Treatises	135
Extrinsic Evidence	137
Impeachment of One's Own Witness	139
Memory and Perception	141
Prior Convictions	143
Prior Inconsistent Statements	146
Specific Instances of Misconduct	148
Insurance Against Liability	149
Judicial Notice	151
Lay Opinion Evidence	153
Leading Questions	155
Misquoting the Witness	157
Narratives	158
Non-Responsive Answers	160
Objections	161
Offers of Proof	162
Original Document Rule	164
Payment of Medical and Similar Expenses	167
Presumptions	168
Privileges	170
Refreshing Present Recollection	172
Relevance	
Generally	174
Conditional Relevance	176
Exclusion of Relevant Evidence on Grounds of Prejudice, Confusion, or Waste of Time	180
Limited Admissibility	182

Rule of Completeness 184
Subsequent Remedial Measures 186

Preface

The following text is designed to provide the practitioner and student with a convenient reference for raising trial objections and presenting responses. This pocket-sized reference book affords the user the opportunity to instantly consult the relevant section of the Illinois Statutes or Illinois Supreme Court Rules, which are reproduced in their entirety in the last section of the book.

The material is presented in alphabetical order; tabs are located on the edges of the pages to aid in locating the appropriate section. Responses are found on the same pages/sections as the objections.

The cross-reference to the applicable Illinois case law follows the objections and responses and an "Explanation" paragraph concludes each topic. This explanatory segment is designed to alert the reader to a practice tip or legal interpretation crucial to proper understanding of the subject matter of that section.

This book is not designed to provide an in-depth analysis of evidentiary rulings or the application of the theories concerning the admission or exclusion of evidence. Instead, *Illinois Evidence with Objections* was developed to furnish users with a complete reference of trial objections and responses, and is small enough to be easily carried to the courtroom or the classroom. We hope you find this material assists you in the pursuit of improving your litigation skills.

National Institute for Trial Advocacy

Ambiguous Questions

Objection

- *I object that the question is* (ambiguous–vague–unintelligible).

Response

In most circumstances it is better to rephrase the question unless counsel is certain of the question's clarity.

Cross-Reference to Illinois Law

People v. Ward, 19 Ill. App. 3d 383, 313 N.E.2d 314 (1974) (ambiguous questions are objectionable). See EDWARD W. CLEARY & MICHAEL H. GRAHAM, HANDBOOK OF ILLINOIS EVIDENCE § 611.26 (6th ed. 1994).

Explanation

An ambiguous question is one that is susceptible to at least two interpretations, or that is so vague or unintelligible as to make it likely to confuse the jury or witness.

Argumentative Questions

Objections

- *I object. The question is argumentative.*
- *I object. Counsel is arguing to the jury.*

Response

- *I am trying to elicit evidence from the witness.*

Cross-Reference to Illinois Law

People v. Clay, 27 Ill. 2d 27, 187 N.E.2d 719 (1963) ("In other words, you did it for the good of the country, is that correct?"). See EDWARD W. CLEARY & MICHAEL H. GRAHAM, HANDBOOK OF ILLINOIS EVIDENCE § 611.23 (6th ed. 1994).

Explanation

An argumentative question is one which does not seek information from the witness but rather makes an argument to the jury in the guise of a question.

Asked and Answered Questions

Objections

- *I object. The question has been asked and answered.*
- *I object. The witness has already answered that question.*

Responses

- *The witness has not yet answered the question.*
- *The question has not been answered during my examination.*

Cross-Reference to Illinois Law

People v. Abrams, 260 Ill. App. 3d 566, 631 N.E.2d 1312 (1994) (general rule). See EDWARD W. CLEARY & MICHAEL H. GRAHAM, HANDBOOK OF ILLINOIS EVIDENCE § 611.24 (6th ed. 1994).

Explanation

A question may be objected to as "asked and answered" when it calls for the repetition of testimony from a witness who has previously given the same testimony in response to a question asked by examining counsel. It is designed to prevent cumulative evidence through repetition of testimony.

Assuming Facts Not in Evidence

Objection

- *I object. The question assumes a fact not in evidence. There has been no testimony that* (insert facts that have been assumed).

Responses

- *I will elicit that fact from the witness in a separate question.*
- *That fact has been proved during the earlier testimony of this witness.*
- *That fact has been proved during the testimony of* (insert the name of another witness who has already testified).
- *This fact will be testified to during the testimony of* (insert the name of another witness who will testify later).

Cross-Reference to Illinois Law

People v. Enis, 139 Ill. 2d 264, 564 N.E.2d 1155 (1990) (general rule; direct examination); People v. Nuccio, 43 Ill. 2d 375, 253 N.E.2d 353 (1969) (cross-examination). See EDWARD W. CLEARY & MICHAEL H. GRAHAM, HANDBOOK OF ILLINOIS EVIDENCE § 611.21 (6th ed. 1994).

Explanation

A question is objectionable if it assumes, in the asking, facts that have not already been proved. The danger is that the jury will accept the facts as stated in the question regardless of the witness's answer. The prohibition governs both direct and cross-examination.

Authentication of Writings, Photographs, and Recordings

Objection

- *I object. This exhibit has not been authenticated.*

Responses

- *This instrument has been authenticated by stipulation of counsel.*
- *The instrument has been authenticated through the testimony of* (insert name of witness) *who has testified that:*
  - *the witness created the writing, or*
  - *the witness was present when the writing was created and testified that it is in substantially the same condition as at the time of its creation, or*
  - *the witness knows the handwriting because (s)he saw the author write or sign the instrument, or*
  - *the witness knows the handwriting from having seen the author sign at another time, or*
  - *the witness knows the handwriting by circumstantial evidence* (state such circumstantial evidence), *or*

- *(where document is proved by an expert witness) the expert has compared the handwriting in question with an authentic handwriting exemplar and that the expert's opinion to a reasonable degree of certainty is that the handwriting in question is that of* (insert name of purported author), or
- *the witness was present at the time the tape recording, audio, or video, was made,* or
- *the witness saw the scene or items portrayed in the photograph at a relevant time and that the photograph is a fair and accurate representation of what was seen,* or
- *the document is self-authenticating as a (newspaper, official publication, certified copy of public record, etc.).*

- *I request the court compare the handwriting in question with an admittedly authentic handwriting exemplar and find that it is the handwriting of* (insert name of purported author).

Cross-Reference to Illinois Law

Illinois permits authentication in a variety of ways, as the responses above show:

> Witness with personal knowledge—People v. Knade, 252 Ill. App. 3d 682, 625 N.E.2d 172 (1993)

Non-expert opinion on identification of handwriting—People v. Williams, 274 Ill. App. 3d 598, 653 N.E.2d 899 (1995)

Comparison by trier or expert—Rogers v. Tyley, 144 Ill. 652, 32 N.E. 393 (1892). See also 735 ILCS 5/8-1501 to 5/8-1503

Circumstantial evidence—Distinctive characteristics—People v. Towns, 157 Ill. 2d 90, 623 N.E.2d 269 (1993)

Self-authentication—People v. Brown, 194 Ill. App. 3d 958, 553 N.E.2d 712 (1990) (public records); 735 ILCS 5/8-1202–1205; 305 ILCS 5/10-13.4 (certain public records); Alimissis v. Nanos, 171 Ill. App. 3d 1005, 525, N.E.2d 1133 (1988) (newspapers and periodicals)

Standard of Proof—Marvel Engineering v. Commercial Union Insurance Co., 118 Ill. App. 3d 844, 455 N.E.2d 545 (1983) (adopts Fed. R. Evid. standard).

See EDWARD W. CLEARY & MICHAEL H. GRAHAM, HANDBOOK OF ILLINOIS EVIDENCE §§ 901, 902 (6th ed. 1994).

Explanation

Before an instrument can be accepted in evidence, the proponent must establish its identity and authorship by stipulation, circumstantial evidence, or the testimony of a witness with knowledge of its identity and authorship. Authentication requires proof "sufficient to support a finding" that the writing is what its proponent claims it to be (Marvel Engineering v. Commercial Union Insurance Co., *supra*). This is the same standard set forth in Federal Rule of Evidence 901.

Authentication of Telephone Conversation and Voices

Objections

- *I object. The telephone conversation has not been authenticated.*
- *I object. The participants in the telephone conversation have not been properly identified.*

Responses

- *The identity of the participants in the telephone conversation has been established through the testimony of* (insert name of witness) *who has testified that:*
  - *the witness is familiar with and recognized the voice,* or
  - *the witness called the number listed to* (insert name of participant) *and the other party identified himself or herself as* (insert name of participant), or
  - *the witness called the number listed to* (insert name of participant) *and the content of the conversation showed* (insert name of person) *to be the person who answered the call,* or
  - *the witness called the number listed to* (insert name of business) *and the conversation*

related to business conducted by (insert name of business) *over the telephone,* or

- (where proof is established by expert witness testimony) *the expert has compared the voice in question with an authentic voice exemplar and that the expert's opinion to a reasonable degree of certainty is that the voice in question is that of* (insert name of purported speaker).

Cross-Reference to Illinois Law

People v. Metcoff, 392 Ill. 418, 64 N.E.2d 867 (1946) (voice identification); People v. Poe, 21 Ill. App. 3d 457, 459 N.E.2d 667 (1984) (contents of statement or reply technique suffice); Tomaszewski v. Godbole, 174 Ill. App. 3d 639, 529 N.E.2d 260 (1988) (regarding calls made <u>by</u> witness, adopts Fed. R. Evid. 901(b)(6)). See EDWARD W. CLEARY & MICHAEL H. GRAHAM, HANDBOOK OF ILLINOIS EVIDENCE § 901.7 (6th ed. 1994).

Explanation

Authentication of telephone conversations and voices is the process of proving the identity of the persons involved in the conversation. Before testimony can be had that a telephone conversation occurred, testimony must be elicited to prove the identity of the participants in the conversation.

Character Evidence: Generally

Objection

- *The question calls for (or the answer provides) evidence of character offered on propensity.*

Response

- *This evidence is:*
  - *offered on propensity by the defendant to show his own pertinent good character,* or
  - *offered on propensity by the prosecution to show a pertinent character trait of the victim,* or
  - *offered for a relevant, non-propensity purpose,* or
  - *offered to prove propensity where character is an essential element of a claim, charge, or defense,* or
  - *offered to impeach the witness.*

Cross-Reference to Illinois Law

Crose v. Rutledge, 81 Ill. 266 (1876) (general common law rule). See EDWARD W. CLEARY & MICHAEL H. GRAHAM, HANDBOOK OF ILLINOIS EVIDENCE § 404.1 (6th ed. 1994).

Explanation

The evidence of a person's character is generally inadmissible as irrelevant when offered on the issue of that person's propensity to act in conformity with such character trait. When a criminal defendant puts in issue his or her own character, or the character of the alleged victim, or where the character of a party is an essential element of a claim, charge, or defense in either the criminal or civil context, character evidence is admissible to show propensity. "Put in issue" means offering evidence, in the form of reputation (and sometimes specific acts) of one's character trait, or of the character trait of the victim. It does not mean relying on a particular affirmative defense, such as self-defense in homicide, or consent in criminal sexual assault.

Character Evidence: Parties in a Civil Case

Objection

- *I object. The question calls for (or the answer provides) evidence of character offered on propensity.*

Responses

- *The evidence is admissible to establish an essential element of a claim, charge, or defense.*
- *The evidence is admissible because the claim (or counter-claim) alleges criminal behavior.*

Cross-Reference to Illinois Law

Consolidated Coal Co. v. Seniger, 179 Ill. 370, 53 N.E. 733 (1899); People v. Moretti, 6 Ill. 2d 494, 129 N.E.2d 709 (1955); McCleary v. Board of Fire & Police Commissioners of the City of Woodstock, 251 Ill. App. 3d 988, 622 N.E.2d 1257 (1993) (admissible where inquiry is essentially into criminal behavior). See EDWARD W. CLEARY & MICHAEL H. GRAHAM, HANDBOOK OF ILLINOIS EVIDENCE § 405.3 (6th ed. 1994).

Explanation

Some causes of action under Illinois law include a character trait as an element. For example, a claim of negligence in employing an incompetent person requires proof that the person is incompetent, a character trait (Consolidated Coal Co. v. Seniger, *supra*). In such cases "character offered on propensity" is admissible. Proof may be in the form of specific instances as well as by reputation in this circumstance, but opinion evidence is not permissible (People v. Moretti, *supra*). Federal Rule of Evidence 405 permits proof by opinion as well as by reputation and specific acts when a character trait is an element.

The Illinois Appellate Court has permitted character evidence to show propensity in a civil case where the gravamen of the complaint was an allegation of criminal behavior (McCleary v. Board of Fire & Police Commissioners of the City of Woodstock, *supra*). In such a case the "criminal rules" apply. (See Character Evidence: Accused or Victim in a Criminal Case, p. 16, *infra*.)

Character Evidence: Accused or Victim in a Criminal Case

Objections

- *I object. The prosecution is attempting to offer evidence of the defendant's character where the defendant has not offered any character evidence.*

- *I object. The prosecution is attempting to offer evidence of the victim's character where none has been offered by the defendant.*

Responses

- *The defendant has opened the door on his or her character by offering evidence of his or her pertinent character trait.*

- *The defendant has opened the door on the victim's character by offering evidence of the victim's character.*

Cross-Reference to Illinois Law

People v. Lewis, 25 Ill. 2d 442, 185 N.E.2d 254 (1962); People v. Whiters, 204 Ill. App. 3d 334, 562 N.E.2d 325 (1990). See EDWARD W. CLEARY &

MICHAEL H. GRAHAM, HANDBOOK OF ILLINOIS EVIDENCE § 404.3 (6th ed. 1994).

Explanation

In a criminal case, Illinois follows the basic common law rules which preclude character evidence unless the defendant offers such evidence first and the evidence is of a pertinent trait of either the accused or the victim. If the defendant offers such evidence, the prosecution may rebut. The prosecution, therefore, cannot be the first to offer character evidence (People v. Lewis, *supra*). Even in a homicide case where the defendant claims that the victim was the first aggressor, the prosecution cannot resort to character evidence unless and until the defendant has offered it. This is contrary to the Federal Rule, which would permit the prosecution to go first in this instance. The Illinois Appellate Court has held, however, that a defendant's opening statement claiming self-defense enables the prosecution to offer character evidence of the victim's peaceableness in its case in chief (People v. Whiters, *supra*).

The admissibility of character evidence in a criminal case is thus governed by rules of timing (defendant goes first usually) and by rules of form (evidence in the form of reputation, usually; specific instances, rarely; opinion, never).

Character Evidence: Accused or Victim in a Criminal Case: Specific Instances

Objection

- *I object. The defendant is offering evidence of the victim's character by showing specific instances of violent behavior.*

Response

- *Specific instances are a proper form of character evidence since we are interposing the affirmative defense of self-defense.*

Cross-Reference to Illinois Law

People v. Randle, 147 Ill. App. 3d 621, 498 N.E.2d 732 (1986) (when defendant relies upon affirmative defense, he may resort to proving character of victim for violence by showing specific instances of violent behavior by victim). See EDWARD W. CLEARY & MICHAEL H. GRAHAM, HANDBOOK OF ILLINOIS EVIDENCE § 404.4 (6th ed. 1994).

Explanation

A defendant's resort to specific instances in this context is contrary to Federal Rule of Evidence 405, which limits the form of proof to reputation or opinion. Note: Specific acts of violent behavior by the victim in a self-defense case, if known to the defendant, may be relevant to the defendant's state of mind, apart from their relevance to the character of the victim.

Character Evidence: Other Acts, Crimes, or Wrongs

Objection

- *I object. This evidence is inadmissible character evidence offered on propensity.*

Response

- *This evidence is not offered on propensity, but rather for the purpose of showing* (state purpose), *a relevant, non-propensity purpose.*

Cross-Reference to Illinois Law

People v. Middleton, 38 Ill. App. 3d 984, 350 N.E.2d 223 (1976) (common design); People v. Lucas, 132 Ill. 2d 399, 548 N.E.2d 1003 (1989) (specific intent); People v. Barbour, 106 Ill. App. 3d 993, 436 N.E.2d 667 (1982) (modus operandi, distinguished from common plan); People v. Romero, 66 Ill. 2d 325, 362 N.E.2d 288 (1977) (cannot use other crimes solely to bolster credibility of witness). People v. Oaks, 169 Ill. 2d 409, 662 N.E.2d 1328 (1996) (standard of proof). See EDWARD W. CLEARY & MICHAEL H. GRAHAM, HANDBOOK OF ILLINOIS EVIDENCE § 404.5 (6th ed. 1994).

Explanation

The Illinois rule is liberal: <u>any</u> relevant purpose. If the evidence has a relevant purpose, it is admissible so long as the prosecution establishes a sufficient foundation to support the inference that the defendant committed the other crime. The foundation does not require proof beyond a reasonable doubt, but it must be greater than mere suspicion (People v. Oaks, *supra*) (compare Huddleston v. United States, 485 U.S. 681 (1988) (the Supreme Court prescribes a sufficiency standard of proof for admissibility of other crimes evidence under Federal Rule of Evidence 404(b)). Note: There is at least one limitation on this kind of proof. The prosecution may not resort to proof of defendant's other crimes solely to bolster the credibility of its witness (People v. Romero, *supra*).

Character Evidence: Prior Sexual Activity of Alleged Victim
(The Rape Shield)

Objections

Civil Cases

> See Character Evidence: Generally

Criminal Cases

- (Opinion or reputation evidence) *I object. The question calls for opinion or reputation evidence concerning the victim's sexual behavior or sexual predisposition.*

- (Specific instances of conduct) *I object. The question calls for evidence concerning the victim's sexual conduct or sexual predisposition and is irrelevant.*

Responses

Civil Cases

> See Character Evidence: Generally

Criminal Cases

- (Reputation evidence and specific instances of conduct)

- *The evidence of sexual behavior is admissible:*
  - *to prove the past sexual conduct of the alleged victim with the accused, because the accused claims the victim consented to the sexual conduct with respect to which the offense is alleged,* and
  - *we ask your honor to entertain our offer of proof in camera where we will establish that we have evidence to impeach the witness in the event that prior sexual activity with the defendant is denied. Also, we will offer specific information as to date, time, or place, or some combination thereof, and we will establish that the evidence is relevant and that its probative value outweighs the danger of unfair prejudice .*

Cross-Reference to Illinois Law

725 ILCS 5/115-7; People v. Sales, 151 Ill. App. 3d 226, 502 N.E.2d 1221 (1987) (prosecution prohibited from showing victim had not had sexual relations with anyone in ten days before attack); People v. Newman, 123 Ill. App. 3d 43, 462 N.E.2d 731 (1984) (Cross-examination to establish prostitution as showing lack of credibility prohibited); People v. Gorney, 107 Ill. 2d 53, 481 N.E.2d 675 (1985) (evidence of previous false allegation of rape admissible). See EDWARD W. CLEARY &

MICHAEL H. GRAHAM, HANDBOOK OF ILLINOIS EVIDENCE § 404.4 (6th ed. 1994).

Explanation

This Illinois Rape Shield statute applies only in criminal prosecutions for sexual assault. It governs proof by <u>both</u> prosecution and defense (People v. Sales, *supra*). The Rape Shield statute permits proof by either specific instances or reputation, when the admissibility criteria are met. The statute limits this reputation and specific act evidence to the relationship between the victim and the accused. Evidence of conduct with others than the accused, and evidence of chastity, generally are not admissible (People v. Newman, *supra*).

The statutory phrase "constitutionally required to be admitted" means, for example, evidence of sexual behavior with others than the accused offered to impeach the victim, by showing her bias (Olden v. Kentucky 488 U.S. 227 (1988) (accused had constitutional right under Sixth Amendment confrontation clause to question victim about her cohabitation with another, to show her bias in making claim of rape) or evidence of a false allegation of rape to show that allegation here is likewise false (People v. Gorney, *supra*).

Character Evidence: Similar Crimes or Acts in Criminal Sexual Assault Cases: Previous Acts Between Defendant and Victim

Objection

- *I object that this evidence is inadmissible character evidence offered on propensity.*

Response

- *This is evidence of a similar crime of sexual assault offered*
  - *to show the relationship and familiarity of parties (or other specific, relevant purposes such as intent, design or course of conduct, and to corroborate complainant's testimony).*

Cross-Reference to Illinois Law

725 ILCS 5/115-7; People v. Anderson, 225 Ill. App. 3d 636, 587 N.E.2d 1050 (1992) (prior acts between the same parties admissible to show the relationship and familiarity of the parties and to corroborate the complaining witness); People v. Rogers, 324 Ill. 2d 224, 154 N.E.2d 909 (1927) (evidence of sex acts with third persons not admissible to show

familiarity, etc.); People v. Johnson, 239 Ill. App. 3d 1064, 608 N.E.2d 36 (1992) (contra).

Explanation

As noted in the previous section, Character Evidence: Prior Sexual Activity of Alleged Victim (The Rape Shield), *infra* p. 22, 725 ILCS 5/115-7 restricts both prosecution and defense. In this section defendant objects to the prosecution's attempt to show his prior sexual acts with the victim. Cleary and Graham cites several cases, of which People v. Anderson, *supra*, is representative, and 725 ILCS 5/115-7 as supporting prosecution's use of such evidence to show the "relationship and familiarity of the parties and to corroborate the complaining witness."

Before the enactment in 1997 of the statute described in the following section, Character Evidence: Similar Crimes or Acts in Criminal Sexual Assault Cases: Previous Acts of Defendant with Others, p. 28, *infra*, the Illinois law was unsettled as to the admissibility of evidence concerning sexual acts by the accused with third persons (See Cleary and Graham, *supra*). Early authority suggested such evidence could not be used to show propensity to commit sex offenses (People v. Rogers, *supra*). Many later cases (People v. Johnson, *supra*) permitted such evidence to show relationship and familiarity, not propensity generally. As discussed in the next section, the new statute seems to provide a broad rule, permitting the evidence to be used even for propensity.

Character Evidence: Similar Crimes or Acts in Criminal Sexual Assault Cases: Previous Acts of Defendant with Others

Objection

- *I object that this evidence is inadmissible character evidence offered on propensity.*

Response

- *The proffered evidence is admissible under 725 ILCS 5/115-7.3 because:*
  - *It is evidence of the defendant's commission of (one of several enumerated sex offenses, including criminal sexual assault and criminal sexual abuse),* and
  - *It is relevant to (a natural issue in this case)* and
  - *Its probative value outweighs any undue prejudice to the defendant in light of its proximity in time to the charged or predicate offense; the degree of factual similarity to the charged or predicate offense; and other relevant facts and circumstances* (recite facts and circumstances).

Cross-Reference to Illinois Law

725 ILCS 5/115-7.3 (evidence of defendant's previous commission of enumerated sex offenses admissible "for its bearing on any matter to which it is relevant." Judge must weigh probative value against prejudice. Prosecution must give advance notice of its intention to use this evidence. Proof is made by specific instances of conduct. Proof in the form of reputation or expert opinion may be resorted to only after opposing party has used reputation or expert opinion.)

Explanation

This new (1997) statute roughly tracks Federal Rules of Evidence 413–415 and broadens Illinois law regarding admissibility of evidence of defendant's commission of sex offenses against other than the victim (see Character Evidence: Similar Crimes or Acts in Criminal Sexual Assault Case: Previous Acts Between Defendant and Victim, *supra*, p. 25). Although broadening Illinois law, this section is narrower than the Federal Rule in several ways. It enumerates the kinds of cases in which the evidence is admissible. It uses the phrase "commission of another offense or offenses" and enumerates those offenses. Finally, it requires that the judge balance probative value and prejudice and it lists factors to be considered in that balancing: proximity in time to the charged offense; degree of factual similarity; and other relevant facts. The statute permits proof to be in the form of specific instances of conduct, reputation, or expert opinion. The use of expert opinion testimony to establish the commission of the "other crime" has no counterpart in the Federal Rules and is unprecedented in Illinois law. Its meaning awaits development in the cases.

Competence to Testify

Objections

- *I object to the calling of this witness on the ground of incompetence to testify because the witness lacks the ability to* (state relevant reason) *which has been shown on the voir dire of the witness.*

- *I move to strike the witness's testimony and object to further testimony on the ground that the witness is incompetent in that his or her testimony has shown the inability to* (state relevant reason).

Responses

- *The witness is presumed competent and there has been no showing of the inability on the part of the witness to perceive, remember, communicate, or appreciate the oath.*

- *The witness is competent to testify and any questions regarding the witness's testimonial capacity go to the weight of the evidence rather than the competency of the witness.*

Cross-Reference to Illinois Law

725 ILCS 5/115-14; People v. Puhl, 211 Ill. App. 3d 457, 570 N.E.2d 447 (1991) (relevant criteria are: (1) ability of witness to receive correct impressions from her senses, (2) ability to recollect these impressions, (3) ability to understand questions and express answers, and (4) ability to appreciate moral duty to tell the truth). See EDWARD W. CLEARY & MICHAEL H. GRAHAM, HANDBOOK OF ILLINOIS EVIDENCE §§ 601.1–601.8 (6th ed. 1994).

Explanation

Children over the age of 14 are presumed competent to testify; in fact, except in the case of children where this age criterion comes into play, all persons are presumed competent to testify. This means that the "burden" is on the party who is challenging competency to show how on one or more of the relevant criteria the witness is incompetent.

Competence to Testify: The Dead Man's Act

Objection

- *I object. By statute the witness is not competent to testify to any conversation with the deceased (or person under a legal disability) or to any event which took place in the presence of the deceased (or person under a legal disability).*

Responses

- *The witness is not barred by the Dead Man's Act from testifying because:*
  - *the witness is not an adverse party or interested person,* or
  - *the witness is not testifying on his own behalf,* or
  - *the witness will not testify to any conversation with the deceased person or person under legal disability or to any event taking place in such person's presence,* or
  - *the representative of the deceased person or person under a disability has already testified to a conversation with the person or to an event which took place in the person's presence,* or

- *the representative has introduced the deposition of the deceased person or person under a legal disability and the proposed testimony concerns matter within the deposition,* or
- *the proposed testimony concerns the witness's account book or other record or document, and is admissible under 735 ILCS 5/8-401,* or
- *the testimony will relate to the heirship of the decedent.*

Cross-Reference to Illinois Law

735 ILCS 5/8-201, 5/8-401. See EDWARD W. CLEARY & MICHAEL H. GRAHAM, HANDBOOK OF ILLINOIS EVIDENCE §§ 606.1–606.6 (6th ed. 1994).

Explanation

Illinois law creates a special rule of competency in the Dead Man's Act. By its terms it designates as incompetent persons who would testify to conversations with a deceased or legally disabled person, or to an event in such person's presence. Its rationale is "to remove the temptation of a survivor to a transaction to testify falsely and to equalize the positions of the parties" (Cleary and Graham, *supra*). The burden is on the person claiming incompetency under the statute. Failure to object constitutes a waiver. To avoid the impact of the statute the proponent can show, as above, that the proffered testimony is not within the statute or that it is admissible under one or more of the statutory exceptions.

Compound Questions

Objection

- *I object. The question is compound.*

Response

- *I withdraw the question and will ask separate questions.*

Cross-Reference to Illinois Law

No reported cases discussing this objection. See EDWARD W. CLEARY & MICHAEL H. GRAHAM, HANDBOOK OF ILLINOIS EVIDENCE § 611.20 (6th ed. 1994).

Explanation

A compound question asks for two or more items of information at the same time, so that it is impossible to understand the meaning of the answer to the question. Objections to compound questions are best made only when the compound question is likely to mislead the jury to the detriment of objecting counsel's client. Otherwise, the objection merely makes the opponent a better questioner.

By analogy to those cases which find vague and ambiguous questions to be objectionable, compound questions are improper as well. They pose the same vice: jury confusion. (See Ambiguous Questions, *supra*, p. 1.)

Compromise/ Offers of Compromise

Objection

- *I object. The proffered evidence is evidence of compromise negotiations offered on liability and/or damages.*

Responses

- *The evidence is admissible because:*
  - *the claim was not in dispute at the time of the compromise discussions, or*
  - *the evidence is not offered on liability or damages but to show (bias or no undue delay), or*
  - *the evidence is an admission of an independent fact.*

Cross-Reference to Illinois Law

Hill v. Hiles, 309 Ill. App. 321, 32 N.E.2d 933 (1941) (general rule); Khatib v. McDonald, 87 Ill. App. 3d 1087, 410 N.E.2d 266 (1980) (claim must be disputed); In re Marriage of Passiales, 144 Ill. App. 3d 629, 494 N.E.2d 541 (1986) (admission of independent fact is admissible); Boey v. Quaas, 139 Ill. App. 3d 1066, 487 N.E.2d 1222 (1986) (statements used for impeachment to show bias). See EDWARD

W. CLEARY & MICHAEL H. GRAHAM, HANDBOOK OF ILLINOIS EVIDENCE § 408 (6th ed. 1994).

Explanation

Evidence of settlement or of settlement negotiations in a disputed civil claim is inadmissible to prove liability or the amount of the claim. Although in a given case an offer to settle may be probative of a consciousness of liability, public policy favoring settlement precludes such use of the evidence in all cases. Liability must be disputed, however, in order for the exclusionary rule to come into play. If liability is admitted and negotiation pertains only to amount, the exclusionary rule doesn't apply (Khatib v. McDonald, *supra*). Statements constituting admissions of independent facts even if made in the course of settlement negotiations are admissible (In re Marriage of Passiales, *supra*). Also, statements made during negotiations may be used as impeachment to show bias (Boey v. Quaas, *supra*).

Cross-Examination: Generally

Objection

- *I move to strike the direct testimony of the witness because I have not had the opportunity to conduct a full and fair cross-examination. I ask that the jury be instructed to disregard the testimony of the witness.*

Responses

- *The purposes of cross-examination have been substantially completed.*
- *Counsel has waived the right to a full and complete cross-examination by* (insert reasons).

Cross-Reference to Illinois Law

People v. Crawford, 23 Ill. 2d 605, 179 N.E.2d 667 (1962) (cross-examination is a matter of right); Grundy City National Bank v. Myre, 34 Ill. App. 3d 287, 339 N.E.2d 348 (matter of right but extent and scope are within discretion of trial court); Bruner v. Buttell, 83 Ill. 317 (1876) (direct testimony may stand where witness dies before cross, but there are other means of attacking the testimony). See also 735 ILCS 5/2-1102 (adverse examination). See

EDWARD W. CLEARY & MICHAEL H. GRAHAM, HANDBOOK OF ILLINOIS EVIDENCE § 611.10 (6th ed. 1994).

Explanation

As to every witness presented by a party, the adverse party has the right to a full and fair cross-examination. The ordinary remedy for the denial of such right is to have the testimony stricken from the record. The right is not unqualified, nor is exclusion a necessary sanction. If, for example, the witness dies after direct examination and before cross-examination, the court may permit the direct testimony to stand, where the opponent has the possibility of attacking the witness by other means, such as by showing bias or prior inconsistent statements (Bruner v. Battell, *supra*). These alternatives are likelier in civil cases because the right to cross-examine is not derived from a clear constitutional command, as it is in criminal cases. In short, in civil cases the court may treat the witness as if he were a hearsay declarant, and permit his testimony to stand where he is attacked by impeachment evidence (see Hearsay: Attacking and Supporting the Credibility of a Hearsay Declarant, p. 64, *infra*).

Cross-Examination: Scope

Objection

- *I object. The question exceeds the proper scope of cross-examination.*

Responses

- *The subject matter of the question was raised when the witness testified on direct examination that* (insert prior testimony).

- *The question seeks to elicit information that is relevant to the credibility of the witness.*

- *I request the court allow inquiry outside the scope of cross-examination. I will conduct the inquiry of the witness as if on direct examination.*

Cross-Reference to Illinois Law

Kurrack v. American District Telephone Co., 252 Ill. App. 3d 885, 625 N.E.2d 675 (1993) (general rule); Leonardi v. Loyola University of Chicago, 168 Ill. 2d 83, 658 N.E.2d 450 (1995) (trial judge rulings on scope are reviewed under abuse of discretion standard); People v. Maldonado, 193 Ill. App. 3d 1062, 550 N.E.2d 1011 (1989) (failure to provide sufficient latitude constitutes denial of right of confrontation). See EDWARD W. CLEARY & MICHAEL H. GRAHAM, HANDBOOK OF ILLINOIS EVIDENCE § 611.11 (6th ed. 1994).

Explanation

Like Federal Rule of Evidence 611(b), the Illinois law limits cross-examination to the subject matter of direct testimony and to matters affecting credibility. "Subject matter of direct" is a broader concept than matters actually mentioned during direct. If the cross-examiner wants to question on matters beyond the scope she must either ask the court's permission to proceed by conducting a direct (non-leading) examination, or by calling the witness in her own case. Issues concerning the scope of cross-examination are, however, within the sound discretion of the trial judge, and his rulings in this regard are reviewed on appeal under an abuse of discretion standard (Leonardi v. Loyola University of Chicago, *supra*). There is one area where the judge's exercise of discretion will be carefully scrutinized: Defendant in a criminal case must be accorded "wide latitude" in developing bias, motive, or interest of the witness (People v. Maldonado, *supra*).

Exhibits: Demonstrative

Objections

- *I object. The proffered exhibit has not been properly authenticated.*
- *I object. The proffered exhibit has not been shown to be:*
  - *(photographs) a fair and accurate depiction of a relevant scene, or*
  - *(object) a fair and accurate representation of an object in issue.*

Responses

- *The demonstrative exhibit has been authenticated by the testimony of* (insert name of witness). *The witness has testified that:*
  - *(photographs) the exhibit looks like an object in issue, or*
  - *the photograph shows a relevant scene as it appeared at a relevant time and the exhibit is a fair and accurate depiction of that scene, or*
  - *(to-scale models) the exhibit is a fair and accurate representation of a scene or object in issue, but drawn or created to (the appropriate scale) as shown by the testimony of the creator.*

Cross-Reference to Illinois Law

Brennan v. Leshyn 51 Ill. App. 2d 132, 201 N.E.2d 167 (1964) (demonstrative exhibits generally); People v. Donaldson, 24 Ill. 2d 315, 181 N.E.2d 131 (1962) (photographs); Burke v. Toledo, Peoria & Western Railway, 148 Ill. App. 3d 208, 498 N.E.2d 682 (1986) (diagrams generally); People v. Henenberg, 55 Ill. 2d 5, 302 N.E.2d 27 (1973) (model of human head); People v. Brown, 172 Ill. 2d 1, 665 N.E.2d 1290 (1996) (admissibility is a matter of the court's discretion); People v. Jones, 114 Ill. App. 3d 576, 449 N.E.2d 547 (1983) (exclusion justified if exhibit would mislead); Madigan v. Browning Ferris Indus., 61 Ill. App. 3d 842, 378 N.E.2d 568 (1978) (to-scale architectural drawing). See EDWARD W. CLEARY & MICHAEL H. GRAHAM, HANDBOOK OF ILLINOIS EVIDENCE § 401.8 (6th ed. 1994).

Explanation

Typical demonstrative exhibits are photographs, models, drawings, and charts. Demonstrative exhibits are admitted solely to illustrate the witness's testimony. They are not substantive evidence (Brennan v. Leshyn, *supra*). The requirement of authentication of such exhibits is satisfied by evidence sufficient to support a finding that the exhibit is a fair and accurate depiction or representation of something that is in issue in a case. If a model or diagram is offered as "to-scale" then the foundation must include testimony which establishes the accuracy of the scale (Madigan v. Browning Ferris Indus., *supra*).

Since demonstrative exhibits are used to assist a witness in her testimony, their admissibility is a matter of the court's discretion (People v. Brown, *supra*). The court may exclude the exhibit if its use would confuse the jury (People v. Jones, *supra*).

Exhibits: Tangible Objects

Objection

- *I object. The proffered exhibit is incompetent for lack of proper foundation.*

Response

- *I have shown through the testimony of* (insert name of witness) *that:*
  - *he or she perceived the exhibit at a relevant time,* and
  - *the exhibit is the one perceived,* and
  - *it is in substantially the same condition as it was at the relevant time.*

Cross-Reference to Illinois Law

Escher v. Norfolk & W. R. Co., 77 Ill. App. 3d 967, 397 N.E.2d 9 (1979) (requirement of same condition); People v. Winters, 97 Ill. App. 3d 288, 422 N.E.2d 972 (1981) (chain of custody). See EDWARD W. CLEARY & MICHAEL H. GRAHAM, HANDBOOK OF ILLINOIS EVIDENCE §§ 401.4, 901.2 (6th ed. 1994).

Explanation

In order to introduce a tangible object into evidence, the proponent must show that it can be identified by a witness who had knowledge of the tangible object at a relevant time. If the probative value of the object depends upon its having remained in the same condition over a period of time, the foundation must include proof that the object is in the same or similar condition as it was on the relevant occasion (Escher v. Norfolk & W. R. Co., *supra*). A chain of custody is <u>not</u> a necessary part of the foundation of a tangible object unless the object is not readily identifiable or is susceptible to alteration by tampering or substitution (People v. Winters, *supra*).

Exhibits: Writings

Objection

- *I object to the introduction of the exhibit in that there is an improper foundation because:*
  - *it is not relevant,* or
  - *authenticity has not been shown,* or
  - *the original document rule has not been met,* or
  - *the writing is hearsay.*

Response

- *The foundation requirements regarding relevance, authentication, the original document rule, and hearsay have been met through the testimony of* (insert name of witnesses), *who have testified that* (insert portion of the relevant testimony).

Cross-Reference to Illinois Law

Larson v. Commonwealth Edison, 33 Ill. 2d 316, 211 N.E.2d 247 (1965) (original writing rule); see Authentication of Writings, Photographs, and Recordings, p. 6, *supra*; Douglas v. Chicago Transit Authority, 3 Ill. App. 3d 318, 279 N.E.2d 44 (1972) (documents may pose hearsay dangers).

Explanation

In order to introduce a writing in evidence, four foundation requirements must be met. The writing must be shown to be relevant, to be authentic, to meet the requirements of the original document rule, and either to qualify as non-hearsay or to meet an exception to the hearsay rule.

Expert Opinion

Objections

- *I object to the qualification of the witness as an expert.*

- *I object to the admission of expert testimony because the discipline in which the witness purports to qualify will not provide information that is helpful to jury determination or understanding of any fact in issue.*

- *I object to the admission of the witness's opinion because it is beyond the area of expertise in which he or she has been qualified.*

- *I object because the theory or process upon which the expert relies has not been shown to be generally accepted within the scientific community from which it is drawn.*

Responses

- *I have shown that the witness is qualified as an expert in* (insert field of expertise) *through the witness's knowledge, skill, experience, training, or education.*

- *I have shown that the area of expertise in which the witness is qualified is one that will be helpful to the jury in determining* (insert fact or conclusion in issue.)

- *The theory (or process) on which the expert has relied has been shown to be accepted within the appropriate scientific community.*

Cross-Reference to Illinois Law

Illinois Supreme Court Rule 220; People v. Free, 94 Ill. 2d 378, 447 N.E.2d 218 (1983) (burden of qualifying); People v. Novak, 163 Ill. 93, 643 N.E.2d 762 (1994) (qualification is matter of discretion); Leonard v. Pitstick Dairy Lake & Park, 124 Ill. App. 3d 580, 464 N.E.2d 644 (1984) (expert testimony admissible whenever it will assist); People v. Jordon, 103 Ill. 2d 192, 469 N.E.2d 569 (1984) (Illinois follows Frye test requiring proof of general acceptance); Wilson v. Clark, 84 Ill. 2d 186, 417 N.E.2d 1322 (1981) (adopting Fed. R. Evid. 703 and 705). See EDWARD W. CLEARY & MICHAEL H. GRAHAM, HANDBOOK OF ILLINOIS EVIDENCE §702.1–706.1 (6th ed. 1994).

Explanation

Illinois law is an interesting amalgam. On the one hand, the Supreme Court adopted Federal Rules of Evidence 703 and 705, which greatly liberalize admission of expert testimony by permitting the expert to give her opinion without first disclosing the basis for it, and to base her opinion on matters not admissible in evidence if "of a type reasonably relied upon by experts in the field" (Wilson v. Clark, *supra*). On the other hand, the so-called <u>Frye</u> test survives. It requires, as part of the foundation for the admissibility of expert testimony based on a novel scientific principle, theory, or process that the proponent show that such principle, theory, or process is generally accepted in the scientific community from which it is drawn (People v. Jordon, *supra*). The United States Supreme Court has held that <u>Frye</u> no longer applies in Federal courts in Daubert v. Merrill Dow Pharmaceuticals, 113 S.Ct. 2786 (1993). Illinois thus clings to an outdated test, but embraces a modern approach.

Supreme Court Rule 220 defines an expert as a person possessing knowledge of a specialized nature. The proponent must therefore qualify the witness as such a person, but the question of qualification is a matter of trial court discretion (People v. Novak, *supra*). In addition, the proponent must establish that the expert testimony will "assist the trier of fact." Expert testimony is admissible even if it pertains to matters of common knowledge and experience, as long as it will aid the trier of fact (Leonard v. Pistick Dairy Lake & Park, *supra*).

Firsthand Knowledge

Objection

- *I object. There has been no foundation to show the witness has personal knowledge of the matter about which he or she has been asked.*

Response

- *The witness has shown firsthand knowledge of the subject matter of the witness's testimony. A foundation has been laid which demonstrates the witness was in position to know those items about which his or her testimony will be given.*

Cross-Reference to Illinois Law

Northern Illinois Gas Co. v. Vincent DiVito Construction, 214 Ill. App. 3d 203, 573 N.E.2d 243 (1991) (general rule). See EDWARD W. CLEARY & MICHAEL H. GRAHAM, HANDBOOK OF ILLINOIS EVIDENCE § 602 (6th ed. 1994).

Explanation

A witness may testify only as to the matters about which he or she has personal or firsthand knowledge. Lack of personal knowledge makes the witness incompetent to testify as to particular facts.

Generally, the proponent of the witness must lay a foundation on the issue of personal knowledge by offering evidence sufficient to support a finding that the witness had firsthand knowledge of the subject matter about which testimony will be given. This objection is distinct from, but often overlaps with, a hearsay objection—where, for example, the witness reports what someone else said, and lacks firsthand knowledge of the event which is reported.

Guilty Pleas
(Offers of Pleas and Related Statements)

Objection

- *I object. Evidence of plea discussions is inadmissible when offered against a criminal defendant.*

Response

- *Evidence of a criminal defendant's plea of guilty is admissible as an admission.*

Cross-Reference to Illinois Law

People v. Friedman, 79 Ill. 2d 341, 405 N.E.2d 229 (1980); People v. Chrisos, 151 Ill. App. 3d 142, 502 N.E.2d 1158 (1986) (statements made in conjunction with guilty plea not withdrawn are admissible). See EDWARD W. CLEARY & MICHAEL H. GRAHAM, HANDBOOK OF ILLINOIS EVIDENCE § 410.1 (6th ed. 1994).

Explanation

By Supreme Court Rule 402(f) (*supra*) plea discussions, offers to plead, and guilty pleas which are later withdrawn are inadmissible against the person offering to plead or pleading. This exclusionary rule serves to promote plea bargaining (People v. Friedman, *supra*).

A plea which is not withdrawn is admissible as an admission, however, as are statements accompanying the pleas (People v. Chrisos, *supra*). The plea is admissible to show the offender admitted the charge, not as proof that the charges are true. The latter purpose relies on the judgment of conviction on the plea as proof of facts essential to sustain the judgment. This use requires a hearsay exception (see Hearsay Exception: Judgment of Previous Conviction, p. 87, *supra*).

Habit and Routine Practice

Objection

- *I object. This evidence is irrelevant in that it is such an isolated occurrence as to be insufficient to constitute a habit or routine practice.*

Response

- *This evidence is relevant because it shows:*
  - *a consistent habit or routine practice*
  - *which raises a permissible inference that the party or organization likely acted in this case according to the habit or routine practice.*

Cross-Reference to Illinois Law

Bradfield v. Illinois Central Gulf R.R. Co., 115 Ill. 2d 471, 505 N.E.2d 531 (1987) (court adopts Fed. R. Evid. 406); Knecht v. Radiac Abrasives, Inc., 219 Ill. App. 3d 979, 579 N.E.2d 1248 (1991) (defining habit). See EDWARD W. CLEARY & MICHAEL H. GRAHAM, HANDBOOK OF ILLINOIS EVIDENCE § 406.1–406.5 (6th ed. 1994).

Explanation

Evidence of a personal habit or of the routine practice of an organization is admissible as relevant to show that on a specific occasion, such person or organization acted in conformity with the proffered habit or practice. By its nature, habit or routine practice testimony is circumstantial proof that certain conduct, or an act consistent therewith, occurred. Habit is defined as conduct that becomes semiautomatic, invariably regular, and not merely a tendency to act in a given manner (Knecht v. Radiac Abrasives, Inc., *supra*).

In abrogating the common law requirement that there be no eyewitnesses before habit testimony can be admitted, Illinois essentially embraces Federal Rule of Evidence 406 (Bradfield v. Illinois Central Gulf R.R. Co., *supra*).

Hearsay: Generally

Objections

- *I object. The question calls for a hearsay answer.*
- *I move to strike the answer as hearsay.*

Response

- *The statement is not being offered for the truth of the matter asserted, but rather is offered to show the statement was made. The making of the statement is relevant to show:*
  - *the effect on a person who heard the statement, or*
  - *a prior inconsistent statement, or*
  - *the operative facts or a verbal act, or*
  - *the knowledge of the declarant.*

Cross-Reference to Illinois Law

People v. Carpenter, 28 Ill. 2d 116, 190 N.E.2d 738 (1963) (hearsay evidence is testimony in court or written evidence, of a statement made out of court, such statement being offered to show the truth of matters asserted therein and thus resting for its value upon the credibility of the out-of-court asserter).

Explanation

The foolproof hearsay test: Ask the question whether the relevant purpose for offering the out-of-court statement is its truth. If the answer to that question is "yes," the out-of-court statement is hearsay. If the answer to the question is not clearly "yes," ask this next question: "Must the content of the out-of-court statement be believed in order to be relevant?" If yes, the evidence is hearsay.

Hearsay:
Two Persistent, False Concepts in Illinois Law
(sometimes called
"the Cook County hearsay rule")

Objection

- *I object. The question calls for hearsay.*

First <u>False</u> Response

- The statement is not hearsay because the declarant is here present on the witness stand now.

Second <u>False</u> Response

- *The statement is not hearsay because it was made in the presence of the party opponent.*

Cross-Reference to Illinois Law

People v. Spicer, 79 Ill. 2d 173, 402 N.E.2d 179 (1969) (presence of declarant on witness stand doesn't make his out-of-court statements nonhearsay); People v. Carpenter, 28 Ill. 2d 116, 190 N.E.2d 738 (1963) (presence of party against whom statement is offered at the making of the statement is irrelevant to hearsay issue). See EDWARD W.

CLEARY & MICHAEL H. GRAHAM, HANDBOOK OF ILLINOIS EVIDENCE § 801.7 (6th ed. 1994).

Explanation

Two persistent, false concepts in Illinois hearsay law at the trial level are (1) that out-of-court statements are admissible if the declarant is now on the witness stand subject to cross and (2) are admissible if the statement was made in party's presence and is offered against that party. Each of these notions—often referred to as variations of the mythical "Cook County hearsay rule"—is demonstrably contrary to the hearsay rationale. Each has been put explicitly to rest by the Illinois Supreme Court in People v. Spicer and People v. Carpenter, *supra*, respectively.

Hearsay: Attacking and Supporting the Credibility of a Hearsay Declarant

Objection

- *I object. The question seeks to attack the credibility of a person who has not appeared as a witness.*

Response

- *This impeachment of an out-of-court declarant is permissible to the same extent available for a testifying witness.*

Cross-Reference to Illinois Law

People v. Smith, 127 Ill. App. 3d 622, 469 N.E.2d 634 (1984) (general rule); People ex. rel. Korzen v. Chicago, Burlington & Quincy R. Co., 32 Ill. 2d 554, 209 N.E.2d 649 (1965) (requiring foundation). See EDWARD W. CLEARY & MICHAEL H. GRAHAM, HANDBOOK OF ILLINOIS EVIDENCE § 806.1 (6th ed. 1994).

Explanation

Impeachment of an out-of-court declarant is permissible to the same extent available for a testifying witness. Impeachment by prior inconsistent statement of a hearsay declarant is permitted despite the inability to confront the declarant with the inconsistency to afford him or her an opportunity to admit or deny, except when the prior statement of conduct occurs prior to the taking of a deposition offered in evidence at trial. The witness must have been confronted at the deposition (People ex. rel. Korzen v. Chicago, Burlington & Quincy R. Co., *supra*). Impeachment of the hearsay declarant as to bias, interest, prejudice, or improper motive may be accomplished without the usual foundation requirement of denial of the same.

Hearsay: Non-Hearsay Admissions

Objections

- *I object. The question calls for a hearsay answer.*
- *I move to strike the answer as hearsay.*

Responses

- *The statement is not hearsay because I have shown that:*
  - *the statement was made by the party opponent,* or
  - *the statement was made by a person and was adopted by the party opponent as the party's own by his act, conduct, or silence, and is thus, a vicarious admission of the party opponent,* or
  - *the statement was made by an agent authorized to speak on behalf of a party opponent, and is thus a vicarious admission of the party opponent,* or
  - *the statement was made by a person in privity with a party,* or
  - *the statement was made by a co-conspirator of the party opponent during the course of the conspiracy and in furtherance of the conspiracy,*

and thus is a vicarious admission of the party opponent.

Cross-Reference to Illinois Law

Guthrie v. Van Hyfte, 36 Ill. 2d 252, 222 N.E.2d 492 (1967) (party's own statement in his individual capacity); Oak Brook Park Dist. v. Oak Brook Dev. Co., 170 Ill. App. 3d 221, 524 N.E.2d 213 (1988) (Privity-statement of property owner admissible against person who inherited the property under owner's will); Pagel v. Yates, 128 Ill. App. 3d 897, 471 N.E.2d 946 (1984) (adoption by conduct); People v. Cihak, 169 Ill. App. 3d 606, 523 N.E.2d 975 (1988) (adoption by silence); Quincy Trading Post, Inc. v. Department of Revenue, 12 Ill. App. 3d 725, 298 N.E.2d 789 (1973) (statement by person authorized to speak); People v. Schmitt, 131 Ill. 2d 128, 545 N.E.2d 665 (1989) (statements by co-conspirator). See EDWARD W. CLEARY & MICHAEL H. GRAHAM, HANDBOOK OF ILLINOIS EVIDENCE § 802 (6th ed. 1994).

Explanation

Any statement made or adopted by a party directly or "vicariously" is admissible against the party if the statement is relevant and if its probative value is not outweighed by the danger of prejudice. Illinois law differs from Federal Rule of Evidence

801(d)(2)(D) in two respects. It includes the concept of "privity" as supporting a vicarious admission, which the Federal Rule does not. It does not include, however, statements by an agent concerning a matter within the scope of the agency, which the Federal Rule does.

Hearsay:
Non-Hearsay Prior Statements:
Child Sexual Abuse

Objections

- *I object. The question calls for a hearsay answer.*
- *I move to strike the answer as hearsay.*

Response

- *The statement is not hearsay because I have shown that:*
  - *pursuant to 725 ILCS 5/115-10 (or 735 ILCS 5/8-2601) it is testimony by a child victim under the age of 13 or a person who was an institutionalized severely or profoundly mentally retarded person recounting his statement complaining of a sexual act,* or
  - *it is testimony of an out-of-court statement made by such child or institutionalized retarded person describing any complaint of a sexual act or matter or detail pertaining to any act which is an element of an offense which is the subject of a prosecution for a sexual act perpetrated on a child or institutionalized retarded person.*

Cross-Reference to Illinois Law

CS 5/115-10 and 735 ILCS 5/8-2601; People v. Holloway, 177 Ill. 2d 1, 682 N.E.2d 59 (1997) (age criterion and timing of statement).

Explanation

The statements described above are, under 725 ILCS 5/115-10, admissible in a prosecution for a sexual act perpetrated on a child or institutionalized severely or profoundly mentally retarded person so long as the court finds in a hearing conducted outside the presence of the jury that the time, content, and circumstances provide sufficient safeguards of reliability and the child or person either testifies or is legally unavailable and there is corroborative evidence of the act which is the subject of the statement. 735 ILCS 5/8-2601 creates a similar exception for civil cases. "Under the age of 13" has been interpreted by the Supreme Court to mean that statements made by a declarant over the age of 12 concerning sexual abuse that occurred when the declarant was under the age of 13 are not admissible (People v. Holloway, *supra*).

Hearsay:
Non-Hearsay Prior Statements:
Prior Inconsistent Statements
in a Criminal Case

Objections

- *I object. The question calls for a hearsay answer.*
- *I move to strike the answer as hearsay.*

Response

- *The statement is not hearsay because I have shown that:*
  - *pursuant to 725 ILCS 5 / 115-10.1 it is a prior inconsistent statement of a witness subject to cross-examination concerning the statement,* and
  - *the statement was made under oath at a trial, hearing, or other proceeding,* or
  - *it narrates, describes, or explains an event or condition of which the witness had personal knowledge and the statement has been proved to have been written or signed by the witness,* or
  - *the witness acknowledged under oath making the statement,* or

- *I have proved that the statement was accurately tape recorded, video recorded, or recorded by any other similar electronic means.*

Cross-Reference to Illinois Law

725 ILCS 5/115-10.1; People v. Saunders, 220 Ill. App. 3d 647, 580 N.E.2d 1246 (1991). See EDWARD W. CLEARY & MICHAEL H. GRAHAM, HANDBOOK OF ILLINOIS EVIDENCE § 801.9 (6th ed. 1994).

Explanation

The Illinois provision for admitting prior inconsistent statements into evidence is both broader and narrower than its Federal counterpart and model, Federal Rule of Evidence 801(d)(1)(A). It is narrower because it applies only in criminal cases. At the same time it is broader because it includes some statements which are not under oath, namely those proved to have been written or signed by the witness, those acknowledged by the witness under oath, and those which are video or audio taped. With these latter statements, however, 725 ILCS 5/115-10.1 requires that the inconsistent statement describe an event of which the declarant has personal knowledge. This has been interpreted to mean a witness's prior inconsistent statement in which he recounted another person's statement (often, in a criminal case, an accomplice recounting the defendant's confession) is not admissible unless the <u>witness</u> has personal knowledge of what is described in the other person's statement (People v. Saunders, *supra*).

G
H

Hearsay:
Non-Hearsay Prior Statements:
Prior Statements of a Witness
Who Refuses to Testify

Objections

- *I object. The question calls for a hearsay answer.*
- *I move to strike the answer as hearsay.*

Response

- *The statement is not hearsay because I have shown that:*
  - *pursuant to 725 ILCS 5/115-10.2 it is the statement of a witness who persists in refusing to testify concerning the subject matter of the statement despite the court's order to do so,* and
  - *it is evidence of a material fact,* and
  - *it is more probative on the point for which it is offered than any other evidence which I can procure through reasonable effort,* and
  - *the interests of justice will best be served by admission.*

Cross-Reference to Illinois Law

725 ILCS 5/115-10.2.

Explanation

Although the Illinois Supreme Court in People v. Olinger, 176 Ill. 2d 326, 680 N.E.2d 321 (1997) specifically refused to adopt a hearsay "catch-all" provision like Federal Rule of Evidence 804(b)(5), the legislature has partially done so in enacting 725 ILCS 5/115-10.2. The provision makes a witness who refuses to testify despite a court order to do so an unavailable witness. The prior statements of this witness are admissible if the criteria are met. Note these criteria do not include inconsistency or oath. Note as well that the provision further requires advance notice of a party's intention to offer statements under this provision.

Hearsay: Hearsay Within Hearsay

Objections

- *I object. The question calls for hearsay within hearsay.*
- *I move to strike the answer because it contains hearsay within hearsay.*

Response

- *Both statements are admissible because each either comes within a hearsay exception or is non-hearsay.*

Cross-Reference to Illinois Law

Horace Mann Insurance Co. v. Brown, 236 Ill. App. 3d 456, 603 N.E.2d 760 (1992). See EDWARD W. CLEARY & MICHAEL H. GRAHAM, HANDBOOK OF ILLINOIS EVIDENCE § 805 (6th ed. 1994).

Explanation\

In order to admit hearsay within hearsay, the proponent must account for both out-of-court statements with either a hearsay exception, or an argument that the out-of-court statement is offered for a relevant, non-hearsay purpose.

Hearsay Exception: Absence of Entry in Business Records

Objections

- *I object. The question calls for hearsay.*
- *I move to strike the answer as hearsay.*

Response

- *The absence of an entry in this record is admissible to show the nonoccurrence of an event. I have shown through the testimony of* (insert name of witness), *who is the custodian of the business records, or other qualified person that:*
  - *a business record exists,* and
  - *the matter which is not recorded in the record is of a kind for which a record would regularly be made and preserved,* and
  - *the source of the information or other circumstances fail to indicate a lack of trustworthiness.*

Cross-Reference to Illinois Law

Easley v. Apollo Detective Agency, Inc., 69 Ill. App. 3d 920, 387 N.E.2d 1241 (1979). See EDWARD W. CLEARY & MICHAEL H. GRAHAM, HANDBOOK OF ILLINOIS EVIDENCE § 803.15 (6th ed. 1994).

Explanation

If the proponent is able to lay a foundation for a record of regularly conducted activity, testimony or the offer of the record for the purpose of demonstrating that a particular entry does not appear in the record is permitted for the purpose of proving that the event, about which the record would have been made, did not occur.

G
H

Hearsay Exception: Absence of Public Records or Entry

Objections

- *I object. The question calls for a hearsay answer.*
- *I move to strike the answer as hearsay.*

Response

- *Evidence of a diligent but unavailing search of the records of the public agency or office is admissible. I have shown through a certification or through the testimony of* (insert name of witness) *that:*
  - *a public agency or office regularly makes and preserves records of a particular kind of matter,* and
  - *a diligent but unavailing search of such records failed to disclose a record, report, statement, data compilation, or entry regarding a particular alleged happening of such a matter.*

Cross-Reference to Illinois Law

People v. Love, 310 Ill. 581, 142 N.E. 204 (1923) (certifications of Secretary of State prepared in accordance with statute admitted to show failure to file documents required by Securities Law). See EDWARD D. CLEARY & MICHAEL H. GRAHAM, HANDBOOK OF ILLINOIS EVIDENCE § 803.15 (6th ed. 1994).

Explanation

The absence of a public record or entry concerning an event that would normally be the subject of a public record is admissible to prove that the event did not occur. A certification by a public agency as to the lack of a record of entry is a means of proving the lack of entry.

Hearsay Exception: Excited Utterance
(or Spontaneous Declaration)
(But Not Present Sense Impression)

Objections

- *I object. The question calls for a hearsay answer.*
- *I move to strike the answer as hearsay.*

Response

- *The statement is admissible as an excited utterance (or spontaneous declaration). I have shown through the testimony of* (insert name of witness) *that the statement:*
  - *relates to a startling event or condition,* and
  - *the event was sufficiently startling to produce a spontaneous and unreflecting statement,* and
  - *there was no time to fabricate.*

Cross-Reference to Illinois Law

People v. Smith, 152 Ill. 2d 229, 604 N.E.2d 858 (1992). See EDWARD W. CLEARY & MICHAEL H. GRAHAM, HANDBOOK OF ILLINOIS EVIDENCE § 803.3 (6th ed. 1994).

Explanation

The rationale of reliability is the absence of time to fabricate, hence the designation "spontaneous" declaration. Yet the cases are numerous in which a lapse of time between the event and the statement—in one case 18 hours—has not precluded use of the exception. The approach has been to look at the totality of circumstances. Thus, statements made in response to direct questions may also be admissible.

Note: Illinois law does not recognize a "present sense impression" exception as does Federal Rule of Evidence 803(2). The spontaneous declaration exception is the closest thing to it, but it differs profoundly in requiring both a startling event and in permitting a significant lapse of time between the event and the declaration.

Hearsay Exception: Family Records

Objections

- *I object. The question calls for a hearsay answer.*
- *I move to strike the answer as hearsay.*

Response

- *This statement is admissible as a family record. I have shown through the testimony of* (insert name of witness) *that this is a statement of fact:*
  - *concerning personal or family history,* and
  - *contained in family Bibles, genealogies, or the like,* and
  - *the declarant is unavailable,* and
  - *the statement was made before the controversy or a motive to misrepresent arose,* and
  - *the declarant is related by blood or marriage to the family.*

Cross-Reference to Illinois Law

Gorden v. Gorden, 283 Ill. 182, 119 N.E. 312 (1918). See EDWARD W. CLEARY & MICHAEL H. GRAHAM, HANDBOOK OF ILLINOIS EVIDENCE § 804.9 (6th ed. 1994).

Explanation

Statements of personal or family history contained in volumes or in other places where, if they were inaccurate, would have been corrected, are admissible to prove the content of those statements. In requiring unavailability, timing, and blood relation, Illinois law preserves common law prerequisites eliminated by Federal Rule of Evidence 803(13).

Hearsay Exception: Former Testimony

Objections

- *I object. The question calls for a hearsay answer.*
- *I move to strike the answer as hearsay.*

Response

- *The statement is admissible as former testimony. I have shown through the testimony of* (insert name of witness) *that:*
  - *the declarant is unavailable,* and
  - *the statement is testimony given as a witness at another hearing of the same or different proceeding, or in an evidence deposition in a civil case, or in a criminal proceeding,* and
  - *the actions are the same or involve the same issues,* and
  - *the parties are the same or (in civil cases) are in privity.*

Cross-Reference to Illinois Law

McInturff v. Insurance Co. of North America, 248 Ill. 92, 93 N.E.2d 369 (1910) (strict requirement of mutuality and same issues). See EDWARD W.

CLEARY & MICHAEL H. GRAHAM, HANDBOOK OF ILLINOIS EVIDENCE § 804.2–804.5 (6th ed. 1994).

Explanation

Former testimony is any testimony given under oath in an earlier proceeding. It is admissible at a later hearing if the declarant is unavailable, and the party against whom it is now offered is the same party who was in the earlier proceeding. In a civil case the testimony may be offered against someone in privity with the party in the earlier proceeding. Privity is strictly interpreted. Examples are owner and bailee, and grantee and grantor. In addition, the issues must be the same in the earlier and current proceedings. The emphasis in Illinois law on privity in civil cases and on identity of issues is contrary to the modern trend, embodied in Federal Rule of Evidence 804(b)(1), which requires only that the person against whom the testimony is now offered have had the opportunity on the former occasion to develop the testimony with a similar motive to that which would animate cross-examination in the current proceeding.

Hearsay Exception: Judgment of Previous Conviction

Objections

- *I object. The question calls for a hearsay answer.*
- *I move to strike the answer as hearsay.*

Response

- *This statement is admissible as a judgment of previous conviction. I have shown through a certified record, or the testimony of* (insert name of witness) *that this statement is evidence of:*
  - *a final judgment,*
  - *entered after a trial or upon a plea of guilty,*
  - *adjudging a person guilty of a serious crime,*
  - *which is offered to prove a fact essential to sustain the judgment,* and
  - *is offered against the convicted person who is a party in this, a subsequent civil suit.*

Cross-Reference to Illinois Law

Smith v. Andrews, 54 Ill. App. 2d 51, 203 N.E.2d 160 (1965). See also In Re Marriage of Engelbach, 181 Ill. App. 3d 563, 537 N.E.2d 372 (1989) (exception applies even where the conviction is not of a party in the subsequent civil suit). See EDWARD W. CLEARY & MICHAEL H. GRAHAM, HANDBOOK OF ILLINOIS EVIDENCE § 803.21 (6th ed. 1994).

Explanation

Illinois law requires that the judgment of conviction be for a "serious crime." Any felony qualifies as serious. Some misdemeanors may as well. Battery has been held to be a serious crime. Traffic offenses are generally considered not to be serious. Federal Rule of Evidence 803(22), in contrast, is concrete: it requires that the judgment of conviction be for a crime punishable by death or imprisonment in excess of one year.

Hearsay Exception: Market Reports and Mortality Tables

Objection

- *I object. The document is an out-of-court statement and is therefore hearsay.*

Response

- *This statement is admissible as a market report or a mortality or annuity table. I have shown the document is:*
  - *a market report admissible under 810 ILCS 5/2-724 (the Uniform Commercial Code) as a report in an official publication, trade journal,* or
  - *in newspapers or periodicals of general circulation published as the reports of such established commodity market,* or
  - *the document is a mortality or annuity table which I have shown to be a standard authority.*

Cross-Reference to Illinois Law

810 ILCS 5/2-724; Alimissis v. Nanos, 171 Ill. App. 3d 1005, 525 N.E.2d 1133 (1988) (published stock

market quotations); Sherman v. City of Springfield, 111 Ill. App. 2d 391, 250 N.E.2d 537 (1969) (life expectancy judicially noticed). See EDWARD W. CLEARY & MICHAEL H. GRAHAM, HANDBOOK OF ILLINOIS EVIDENCE § 803.18 (6th ed. 1994).

Explanation

Market reports or commercial publications are out-of-court statements which compile facts or data used by either the general public or by persons in particular professions or occupations and which are relied upon for the purposes of carrying out their daily businesses. The Uniform Commercial Code makes certain official reports admissible as reports of established commodity markets. Mortality and annuity tables are admissible to show life expectancy when they are established as standard authorities, by expert testimony or by resort to judicial notice.

Hearsay Exception: Birth, Baptismal, and Similar Certificates

Objection

- *I object. The document is an out-of-court statement offered for its truth and is hearsay.*

Response

- *This statement is admissible as a birth, baptismal, or similar certificate. I have shown through the testimony of* (insert name of witness) *that this is a statement contained in a regularly kept record of a religious organization concerning facts of personal or family history.*

Cross-Reference to Illinois Law

Daily v. Grand Lodge, 311 Ill. 184, 192 N.E. 478 (1929) (baptismal certificate to prove fact, date, and place of baptism); Ashford v. Ziemann, 99 Ill. 2d 353, 459 N.E.2d 940 (1984) (birth certificate to prove fact, date, and place of birth). See EDWARD W. CLEARY & MICHAEL H. GRAHAM, HANDBOOK OF ILLINOIS EVIDENCE § 803.16 (6th ed. 1994).

Explanation

This obscure exception has, according to Cleary and Graham, *supra*, an "uncertain dimension." A record of baptism has been admitted to show fact of baptism, and that child was adopted, not natural. It has not, however, been admitted as proof of date of birth.

Hearsay Exception: Public Records and Reports

Objections

- *I object. The question calls for a hearsay answer.*
- *I move to strike the answer as hearsay.*

Response

- *The out-of-court statement is admissible under the hearsay exception for public records and reports. I have shown through the testimony of* (insert name of witness) *that:*
  - *the document is a record, kept by a public officer,*
  - *dealing with his official activities,* and
  - *is reasonably necessary for the performance of the duties of the office,* or
  - *contains matters observed pursuant to duty imposed by law as to which matter there was a duty to report.*

Cross-Reference to Illinois Law

People v. Hester, 88 Ill. App. 3d 392, 410 N.E.2d 638 (1980); 725 ILCS 5/115-5.1 (provides hearsay exception in both civil and criminal cases for public records of the coroner's medical or laboratory examiner summarizing the results of an autopsy). See EDWARD W. CLEARY & MICHAEL H. GRAHAM, HANDBOOK OF ILLINOIS EVIDENCE § 803.12 (6th ed. 1994).

Explanation

This exception is "based upon the assumption that public officers will perform their duties, that they lack a motive to falsify and that public inspection to which many records are subject will disclose inaccuracies" (Cleary and Graham, *supra*). The exception does not include, however, opinions and conclusions. In this respect it is narrower than its counterpart in the Federal Rules of Evidence, Rule 803(8)(c). There are no special limitations within this common law rule for its use in criminal cases, but statute and Supreme Court Rule limitations have been created (see Hearsay Exception: Public Records and Reports: Police Reports, p. 95, *infra*).

Hearsay Exception: Public Records and Reports: Police Reports

Objections

- *I object. The question calls for a hearsay answer.*
- *I move to strike the answer as hearsay.*

Response

- *This police report is admissible as a public record or as a business record under 725 ILCS 5/115-5(a). I have shown through the testimony of* (insert name of witness) *that:*
  - *this police report records routine activities, i.e., ministerial, objective, non-evaluative matters, and was made in a non-adversarial setting,* and
  - *otherwise meets the foundation requirements for a public record or business record,* or
  - *is a laboratory report dealing with controlled substances admissible under 725 ILCS 5/115-15.*

Cross-Reference to Illinois Law

Supreme Court Rule 236(b) (excludes in civil cases police accident reports); 725 ILCS 5/115-5(c) (excludes police investigative reports in criminal cases). But see People v. Lacey, 93 Ill. App. 2d 430, 235 N.E.2d 649 (1968) (police radio logs not excluded); People v. Hawthorn, 60 Ill. App. 3d 776, 377 N.E.2d 335 (1978) (county jail address records admitted as public records); 725 ILCS 5/115-15 (laboratory report of contents, weight, and identity of purported controlled substance is prima facie evidence unless the accused demands the testimony of the person signing the report). See EDWARD W. CLEARY & MICHAEL H. GRAHAM, HANDBOOK OF ILLINOIS EVIDENCE § 803.13 (6th ed. 1994).

Explanation

By statute and rule, Illinois law prevents the use of police accident reports or investigative reports as business records or as public records. Police reports are, however, diverse in nature. Some are merely ministerial and routine. They are not "investigative." These truly routine reports are not excluded by Supreme Court Rule 236(b) or by 725 ILCS 5/115-5(c). They are admissible provided the requisite public record or business record foundation is established.

Even investigative reports may be admitted on theories other than public or business records. The police report may be used as the witness's past recollection recorded or it may be used to impeach.

Since police reports often contain multiple hearsay—which accounts in large part for the ban on their general use—the proponent of the report who relies on a theory that the report is the witness's past recollection recorded must have a theory of admissibility for every hearsay statement in the report, not just the maker's own statements.

725 ILCS 5/115-15 creates an additional exception to the general rule of exclusion by providing that a laboratory report of the Department of State Police, Division of Forensic Services and Identification is prima facie evidence of the contents, weight, and identity of a substance, unless the accused demands the presence of the maker of the report.

Hearsay Exception: Recorded Recollection

Objections

- *I object. The question calls for a hearsay answer.*
- *I move to strike the answer as hearsay.*

Responses

- *This statement is admissible as recorded recollection.*
- *I have shown through the testimony of* (insert name of witness) *that it is:*
  - *a memorandum or record concerning a matter,*
  - *about which a witness once had knowledge,*
  - *but now has insufficient recollection, which cannot be refreshed by the memorandum,* and
  - *I have shown the memorandum to have been made or adopted by the witness when the matter was fresh in the witness's memory and to reflect that knowledge correctly.*

Cross-Reference to Illinois Law

Salcik v. Tassone, 236 Ill. App. 3d 548, 603 N.E.2d 793 (1992) (basic rule); People v. Olson, 59 Ill. App. 3d 643, 375 N.E.2d 533 (1978) (document may be admitted as an exhibit). See EDWARD W. CLEARY & MICHAEL H. GRAHAM, HANDBOOK OF ILLINOIS EVIDENCE § 803.9 (6th ed. 1994).

Explanation

Past recollection recorded must be distinguished from present recollection refreshed. (See Refreshing Present Recollection. p. 172, *infra*.) Though both require a failure of memory as a predicate, present recollection refreshed presents no hearsay problem at all. Present recollection refreshed refers to a situation where a witness has a failure of memory. The witness is then shown the item which serves to refresh his or her recollection; the item is then removed from the witness, and the witness testifies from a refreshed recollection. Past recollection recorded refers to a document created by the witness, or at the witness's direction, when the matter was fresh in the witness's mind so as to accurately reflect that knowledge. Under Illinois law the document may be read to the jury or admitted as an exhibit (People v. Olson, *supra*). This is contrary to Federal Rule of Evidence 803(5), which restricts publication to reading the document to the jury, unless the opponent demands that it be admitted as an exhibit.

Hearsay Exception: Records of Regularly Conducted Activity
(Business Records)

Objections

- *I object. The question calls for a hearsay answer.*
- *I move to strike the answer as hearsay.*

Responses

- (Civil case) *This statement is contained in a hospital record which is admissible as a business record pursuant to Illinois Supreme Court Rule 236(b) or 725 ILCS 5/115-5(a). I have shown through the testimony of* (insert name of witness), *who is a custodian of the record or person who has knowledge of the record-keeping system, that the statement is contained in:*

(For manually entered records)

- *a writing or record (in the form of an entry or otherwise),*
- *which was made as a memorandum or record of any act transaction, occurrence, or event,*

- *at the time of such act, transaction, occurrence or event, or within a reasonable time thereafter,* and
- *was made in the regular course of business,* and
- *it was the regular practice of the business to make such record at the time of such act, transaction, occurrence, or event.*

(For computer-generated records, repeat the above steps and add)

- *the particular computer produces an accurate record when properly employed and generated,* and
- *the computer was properly employed and operated in the matter at hand,* and
- *the foundation testimony concerning the sources of information, method, and time of preparation indicates the trustworthiness of the evidence.*

Cross-Reference to Illinois Law

Supreme Court Rule 236(b); 725 ILCS 5/115-5(a); People ex rel. Schacht v. Main Insurance Co., 114 Ill. App. 3d 334, 448 N.E.2d 950 (1983) (basic rule); Preski v. Warchol Construction Co., 111 Ill. App. 3d 641, 444 N.E.2d 1105 (1982) (lack of personal knowledge of maker goes to weight, not admissibility);

Grand Liquour Co. v. Department of Revenue, 67 Ill. 2d 195, 367 N.E.2d 1238 (1977) (computer records). See EDWARD W. CLEARY & MICHAEL H. GRAHAM, HANDBOOK OF ILLINOIS EVIDENCE § 803.10 (6th ed. 1994).

Explanation

Illinois law enunciates the traditional common law business records exception. The Illinois rule does not require that the maker of the entry have personal knowledge of the transaction or occurrence which is recorded. Lack of personal knowledge goes to weight, not admissibility. Opinions are ordinarily not permitted, but the law is unsettled on this point (see People ex rel. Schacht v. Main Insurance Co., *supra*). In the case of computer records, the foundation requirements include authentication of the accuracy of the computer process.

Hearsay Exception: Records of Regularly Conducted Activity
(Hospital Records Offered as Business Records)

Objections

- *I object. The question calls for a hearsay answer.*
- *I move to strike the answer as hearsay.*

Responses

- (Civil case) *This statement is contained in a hospital record which is admissible as a business record pursuant to Supreme Court Rule 236(b) and 725 ILCS 5/115-5(a). I have shown that:*
  - *(establish the normal business record foundation.)*
- (Criminal case) (There is no response.)

Cross-Reference to Illinois Law

Supreme Court Rule 236(b); 725 ILCS 5/115-5(c). See EDWARD W. CLEARY & MICHAEL H. GRAHAM, HANDBOOK OF ILLINOIS EVIDENCE § 803.11 (6th ed. 1994).

Explanation

Traditionally, medical records were not admissible as business records in civil or criminal cases. In 1992 the Illinois Supreme Court amended Rule 236(b) to permit hospital and medical records to be admitted as business records in civil cases. In criminal cases, however, 725 ILCS 5/115-5(c) preserves the ban on such records as business records.

Hearsay Exception: Records of Vital Statistics

Objection

- *I object. The record is an out-of-court statement offered for its truth and is hearsay.*

Response

- *The out-of-court statement is admissible pursuant to 410 ILCS 535/1–535/29 for records of a vital statistic in that it:*
  - *is a record regarding a vital statistic*
  - *which records a report made to a public official required by law to keep such a record.*

Cross-Reference to Illinois Law

410 ILCS 535/1 (requiring birth and death certificates and making contents of such certificates prima facie evidence of facts stated); People v. Fiddler, 45 Ill. 2d 181, 258 N.E.2d 359 (1970) (exception admits facts only, not opinions); Alfaro v. Meagher, 27 Ill. App. 3d 292, 326 N.E.2d 545 (1975) (exception applicable only to matters specifically permitted by the statute to be included). See EDWARD W. CLEARY & MICHAEL H. GRAHAM,

HANDBOOK OF ILLINOIS EVIDENCE § 803.14 (6th ed. 1994).

Explanation

As with other out-of-court writings which are offered pursuant to a hearsay exception, records of vital statistics must be authenticated either through the testimony of the public officer who creates and maintains the records or, more easily, by the proffer of a certified copy of the public record. The Illinois statutory exception is limited to birth and death certificates, excludes opinions, and is applicable only to matters specifically permitted by the statute to be included.

Hearsay Exception: Reputation as to Character

Objections

- *I object. The question calls for a hearsay answer.*
- *I move to strike the answer as hearsay.*

Response

- *This statement is admissible as reputation as to character. I have shown through the testimony of* (insert name of witness) *that this is a statement of:*
  - *reputation of a person's character*
  - *among associates or in the community.*

Cross-Reference to Illinois Law

See Edward W. Cleary & Michael H. Graham, Handbook of Illinois Evidence §§ 803.20, 405 (6th ed. 1994).

Explanation

Reputation is by definition a collection of hearsay. When offered to show what someone's character is, therefore, reputation poses the hearsay dangers, thus necessitating an exception. Cleary and

Graham says that the admissibility of reputation as a hearsay exception is "implicit in the traditional acceptance of reputation to prove character." Note, however, that if the relevance of the evidence is only what the reputation <u>is</u>, as opposed to showing character or the "truth" of the reputation, the evidence does not pose hearsay dangers. The only issue then is whether the proponent has established a sufficient foundation: has she shown that the reputation <u>exists</u>? (See CHRISTOPHER B. MUELLER & LAIRD C. KIRKPATRICK, MODERN EVIDENCE § 8.69 (1995)).

Hearsay Exception: Reputation Concerning Personal or Family History

Objections

- *I object. The question calls for a hearsay answer.*
- *I move to strike the answer as hearsay.*

Response

- *This statement is admissible as a statement of reputation concerning personal or family history. I have shown through the testimony of* (insert name of witness) *that this is a statement of reputation:*
  - *among members of one's family,*
  - *and is based on more than occasional or casual conversation,*
  - *and is offered to prove family history, residences, deaths, or illegitimacy.*

Cross-Reference to Illinois Law

Harland v. Eastman, 107 Ill. 535 (1883) (family history); Sugrue v. Crilley, 329 Ill. 458, 160 N.E. 847 (1928) (reputation must have arisen prior to controversy). See EDWARD W. CLEARY & MICHAEL

H. Graham, Handbook of Illinois Evidence § 803.19 (6th ed. 1994).

Explanation

The common law rule extends beyond reputation in the family to reputation in the community as well to establish death and marriage. The reputation must have existed before the controversy in issue arose.

Hearsay Exception: Requirement of Unavailability for Certain Hearsay Exceptions

Objections

- *I object. The question calls for a hearsay answer.*
- *I move to strike the answer as hearsay.*

Response

- *The out-of-court statement meets* (insert the appropriate exception). *The declarant is unavailable because the declarant:*
  - *is exempted from testifying concerning the subject of the statement by ruling by the court on the ground of privilege,* or
  - *persists in refusing to testify concerning the subject of the statement despite a court order to do so,* or
  - *testifies to a lack of memory on the subject of the statement,* or
  - *is unable to testify at the hearing because of death or illness,* or
  - *is absent from the hearing and I, as the proponent of the declarant's statement, have been unable to procure the declarant's attendance through process or other means,* and

- *I have been unable to depose the declarant.*

Cross-Reference to Illinois Law

People v. Johnson, 118 Ill. 2d 501, 517 N.E.2d 1070 (1987) (adopting unavailability criteria of Fed. R. Evid. 804(a)), Brownlie v. Brownlie, 351 Ill. 72, 183 N.E. 613 (1932) (requires attempt to depose); 725 ILCS 5/115-10.2 (witness who persists in refusal to testify is unavailable). (See Hearsay: Non-Hearsay Prior Statements: Prior Statements of a Witness Who Refuses to Testify, p. 74, *supra*.) See EDWARD W. CLEARY & MICHAEL H. GRAHAM, HANDBOOK OF ILLINOIS EVIDENCE § 804.1 (6th ed. 1994).

Explanation

Unavailability of a hearsay declarant does not, in and of itself, create an exception to the hearsay rule. Unavailability is merely the first requirement for certain exceptions to the hearsay rule. 725 ILCS 5/115-10.2 provides that a witness who refuses to testify despite a court order to do so is unavailable for purposes of that section. (See Hearsay: Non-Hearsay Prior Statements: Prior Statements of a Witness Who Refuses to Testify, p. 74, *supra*.) Although Illinois law essentially tracks Federal Rule of Evidence 804(a) (People v. Johnson, *supra*), there is an important difference. Rule 804(a) requires that as part of the foundation for a showing of unavailability the proponent show that she could not depose the declarant. This applies to all the exceptions which require a showing of unavailability except former testimony (where it would be superfluous). Illinois law requires, however, that even for former testimony the proponent must show she was unable to depose the declarant (Brownlie v. Brownlie, *supra*).

Hearsay Exception: Declaration Against Interest

Objections

- *I object. The question calls for a hearsay answer.*
- *I move to strike the answer as hearsay.*

Response

- *This statement is admissible as a declaration against interest. I have shown through the testimony of* (insert name of witness) *that the statement:*
  - *was made by a declarant who is now unavailable,* and
  - *was at the time of its making, so far contrary to the declarant's pecuniary or proprietary interest,* or
  - *so far tended to subject the declarant to criminal or civil liability,* or
  - *to render invalid a claim by the declarant against another,* and
  - *that a reasonable person in the declarant's position would not have made this statement unless he or she believed it to be true,* and
  - (If the statement tends to expose the declarant to criminal liability and is offered to

exculpate the accused) *corroborating circumstances clearly indicate the trustworthiness of the statement.*

Cross-Reference to Illinois Law

Horace Mann Insurance Co. v. Brown, 236 Ill. App. 3d 456, 603 N.E.2d 760 (1992) (against pecuniary interest); Buckley v. Cronkhite, 74 Ill. App. 3d 487, 393 N.E.2d 60 (1979) (collateral statements included); People v. Bowel, lll Ill. 2d 58, 488 N.E.2d 995 (1986) (adopting "against penal interest," using criteria of Chambers v. Mississippi, 410 U.S. 52 (1973) and citing Fed. R. Evid. 804(b)(3)); People v. Tate, 87 Ill. 2d 134, 429 N.E.2d 470 (1981) (statements offered to exculpate the accused not admissible unless corroborating circumstances clearly indicate trustworthiness); People v. Cruz, 162 Ill. 2d 314, 643 N.E.2d 636 (1994) (even plea bargaining statements may be declarations against interest); Williamson v. United States, 512 U.S. 594 (1994) (collateral statements not admissible under Fed. R. Evid. 804(b)(3)); People v. Wilson, 271 Ill. App. 3d 943, 649 N.E.2d 1377 (1995) (interprets Williamson and implies collateral statements would not be admissible). See EDWARD W. CLEARY & MICHAEL H. GRAHAM, HANDBOOK OF ILLINOIS EVIDENCE § 804.7 (6th ed. 1994), Supplement, p. 219 (Aspen Law & Business, 1997).

Explanation

When an accused offers statements of others to exculpate himself, and asserts that such statements are declarations against penal interest, she must show corroborating circumstances which indicate the reliability of the statements. While the United States Supreme Court has required that every statement which is offered under the against interest exception be itself actually against interest (Williamson v. United States, *supra*), Illinois law is unclear in the wake of People v. Wilson, *supra*, where the court approved admission of certain allegedly against interest statements and distinguished Williamson.

Hearsay Exception: Statements in Ancient Documents

Objection

- *I object. The statement is contained in an out-of-court writing offered for its truth, which is hearsay.*

Response

- *This statement is admissible as a statement contained in an ancient document. I have shown through the testimony of* (insert name of witness) *that the statement is contained in:*
  - *a document affecting real property in existence thirty years or more,*
  - *the authenticity of which I have established through the testimony of* (insert name of witness) *or through* (state other means).

Cross-Reference to Illinois Law

Reuter v. Stuckart, 18 Ill. 529, 54 N.E. 1014 (1899) (exception limited to documents affecting real property). See EDWARD W. CLEARY & MICHAEL H. GRAHAM, HANDBOOK OF ILLINOIS EVIDENCE § 803.17 (6th ed. 1994).

Explanation

The foundation requirements for establishing authenticity of an ancient document require that the condition of the document create no suspicion regarding its authenticity; the document must have been kept in a place where it likely would be kept if it were authentic, and it must have been in existence for at least thirty years at the time of its proffer at trial. Illinois law limits the exception to documents affecting real property.

Hearsay Exception: Statement of Personal or Family History

Objections

- *I object. The question calls for a hearsay answer.*
- *I move to strike the answer as hearsay.*

Response

- *This statement is admissible as a statement of personal or family history. I have shown through the testimony of* (insert name of witness) *that:*
  - *the declarant is deceased,* and
  - *the statement concerns the declarant's own birth, adoption, marriage, divorce, legitimacy, relationship by blood, adoption, or marriage, ancestry or other similar fact of personal or family history,* and
  - *the statement was made before the controversy arose,* and
  - *the declarant was related by blood or marriage to the family to which the declarations refer.*

Cross-Reference to Illinois Law

Daniels v. Retirement Board, 106 Ill. App. 3d 412, 435 N.E.2d 1276 (1982) (general rule); Jarshow v. Grosse, 257 Ill. 36, 100 N.E.2d 290 (1912) (foundation). See EDWARD W. CLEARY & MICHAEL H. GRAHAM, HANDBOOK OF ILLINOIS EVIDENCE § 804.8 (6th ed. 1994).

Explanation

The requirement of declarant's personal knowledge, which ordinarily must be apparent from the circumstances of the making of a declarant's admissible hearsay statement, is dispensed with. Moreover, the declarant's own statement is admissible to prove the relationship in cases where the estate of the declarant herself is sought. Ordinarily, proof of the relationship must be by proof other than the declarant's statement.

Hearsay Exception: Statements for Purposes of Medical Diagnosis or Treatment

Objections

- *I object. The question calls for a hearsay answer.*
- *I move to strike the answer as hearsay.*

Response

- *This statement is admissible as a statement for purposes of medical diagnosis or treatment. I have shown through the testimony of* (insert name of witness) *that the statement:*
  - *was made for purposes of medical diagnosis or treatment,* and
  - *describes medical history; or describes past or present symptoms, pain, or sensations; or describes the inception or general character of the cause or external source thereof,* and
  - *was reasonably pertinent to diagnosis or treatment.*

Cross-Reference to Illinois Law

People v. Winfield, 160 Ill. App. 3d 893, 513 N.E.2d 1032 (1987) (general rule—treating physicians);

People v. Hester, 39 Ill. 2d 489, 237 N.E.2d 466 (1968) (general rule—examining physicians); Wilson v. Clark, 84 Ill. 2d 186, 417 N.E.2d 1322 (1981) (adopting Fed. R. Evid. 703 and 705); People v. Anderson, 113 Ill. 2d 1, 495 N.E.2d 485 (1986) (defendant's statements to a psychiatrist, testifying on behalf of defendant on issue of insanity, may be disclosed to jury where psychiatrist relied upon statement in forming his opinion). See EDWARD W. CLEARY & MICHAEL H. GRAHAM, HANDBOOK OF ILLINOIS EVIDENCE § 803.8 (6th ed. 1994).

Explanation

Statements made to persons other than those immediately able to render medical assistance can qualify for this hearsay exception if made for purposes of obtaining medical diagnosis or treatment. However, statements of causation or the external source of the physical condition mentioned in the out-of-court statement will only be admissible if pertinent to the medical diagnosis or treatment. The key inquiry is whether the statement is pathologically germane to the diagnosis or treatment of a medical patient. Where and how an injury occurs is usually germane; who caused the injury usually is not. Illinois law maintains the distinction between examining and treating physicians, so that this exception does not apply to statements made to a physician for the purpose of preparing the physician to testify. Note, however, that in light of the Supreme Court's adoption of Rule 703 in Wilson v. Clark, *supra*, this distinction may be meaningless. Rule 703 permits the expert to rely on the patient's statements in forming his opinion, and presumably permits as well the physician to divulge these statements to the jury. (See Expert Opinion, *supra*, p. 51.) These statements are not admissible substantively in this situation, however, so a limiting instruction is justified (People v. Anderson, *supra)*.

Hearsay Exception: Statements for Purposes of Medical Diagnosis or Treatment in Sexual Abuse Prosecutions

Objections

- *I object. The question calls for a hearsay answer.*
- *I move to strike the answer as hearsay.*

Response

- *This statement is admissible pursuant to 725 ILCS 5/115-13 as a statement for diagnosis or treatment. I have shown through the testimony of* (insert name of witness) *that:*
  - *the statement was made by a victim in a sexual abuse prosecution to medical personnel for purposes of medical diagnosis and treatment,* and
  - *the statement describes the cause of symptoms, pain, or sensations,* or
  - *the inception or general character of the cause or external source thereof,* and
  - *such descriptions are reasonably pertinent to diagnosis or treatment.*

Cross-Reference to Illinois Law

725 ILCS 5/115-13; People v. Denny, 24 Ill. App. 3d 345, 608 N.E.2d 1313 (1993) (includes identity); People v. Hall, 235 Ill. App. 3d 418, 601 N.E.2d 883 (1992) (does not include identity) (compare Hearsay: Non-Hearsay Prior Statements, Child Sexual Abuse, p. 69, *supra*). See EDWARD W. CLEARY & MICHAEL H. GRAHAM, HANDBOOK OF ILLINOIS EVIDENCE § 803.8 (6th ed. 1994).

Explanation

The apparent purpose behind enactment of 725 ILCS 5/115-13 is to permit introduction in a sexual abuse prosecution of statements by the victim—regardless of age—which identify the offender. The Illinois Appellate Court has reached contradictory conclusions about whether the identity of the offender is included within the exception.

Hearsay Exception: Dying Declaration

Objections

- *I object. The question calls for a hearsay answer.*
- *I move to strike the answer as hearsay.*

Response

- *The statement is admissible as a dying declaration. I have shown through the testimony of* (insert name of witness) *that the statement:*
  - *was made by a declarant who was the victim of the homicide for which the accused is being prosecuted,* and
  - *was made while the declarant believed his death was impending and almost certain to follow immediately,* and
  - *the statement concerned the causes or circumstances of what the declarant believed to be impending death.*

Cross-Reference to Illinois Law

People v. Webb, 125 Ill. App. 3d 924, 466 N.E.2d 936 (1984) (general rule); Marshall v. Chicago & G. E. Ry., 48 Ill. 475 (1868) (exception does not apply in civil cases). See EDWARD W. CLEARY &

Michael H. Graham, Handbook of Illinois Evidence § 804.6 (6th ed. 1994).

Explanation

Illinois law limits the dying declaration exception to homicide cases and requires that the declarant be the victim of the homicide for which the accused is being prosecuted. The accused may, however, offer the statement to exculpate himself.

Hearsay Exception: Then-Existing Mental, Emotional, or Physical Condition

Objections

- *I object. The question calls for a hearsay answer.*
- *I move to strike the answer as hearsay.*

Response

- *This statement is admissible as a statement of a then-existing mental, emotional, or physical condition. I have shown through the testimony of* (insert name of witness) *that the statement:*
  - *is of the declarant's then-existing:*
    state of mind, or
    emotions, or
    sensation, or
    physical condition, or
  - *although it indicates a statement of memory or belief offered to prove the fact remembered or believed, it relates to the execution, revocation, identification, or terms of declarant's will.*

Cross-Reference to Illinois Law

Rizzo v. Rizzo, 95 Ill. App. 3d 636, 420 N.E.2d 555 (1981) (statement of children expressing desire in custody dispute); People v. Bartall, 98 Ill. 2d 298, 456 N.E.2d 59 (1983) (intent); Barton v. Wylde, 261 Ill. 397, 103 N.E. 976 (1914) (fact remembered or believed admissible if it relates to execution, revocation, identification, or terms of will); People v. Reddock, 13 Ill. App. 3d 296, 300 N.E.2d 31 (1973) (statement admissible to show declarant's intent only, not to show what any other person intended). See EDWARD W. CLEARY & MICHAEL H. GRAHAM, HANDBOOK OF ILLINOIS EVIDENCE § 803.4 (6th ed. 1994).

Explanation

It is critical to note that only statements regarding a present mental, emotional, or physical condition fit within the exception. A statement regarding a past mental, emotional, or physical condition will not be admissible because there is no substantial guarantee of reliability, except when the statement relates to the declarant's will. Note that the exception for statements expressing intent offered to show the doing of an act applies only to the declarant's doing of an act. They may not be admitted to prove that some person other than the declarant, to whom the declarant referred in stating his own intent, undertook some future act (People v. Reddock, *supra*).

Impeachment: Bias, Prejudice, Interest, and Improper Motive

Objections

- (To questions posed on cross-examination) *I object. Counsel is attempting to impeach the witness on improper grounds. The testimony attempted to be elicited is irrelevant.*

- (To extrinsic evidence) *I object. Counsel has not laid the proper foundation for use of extrinsic evidence to impeach. The witness whom counsel is attempting to impeach:*
  - *has not yet been called as a witness,* or
  - *was not confronted with the alleged bias, interest, or improper motive on cross-examination,* or
  - *was confronted with the alleged bias, prejudice, interest, or improper motive, but did not deny its existence.*

Responses

- (To an objection posed on cross-examination) *I am attempting to show that the witness:*
  - *is biased,* or
  - *is prejudiced,* or

- *has an interest in the outcome of the case,* or
- *has an improper motive for giving testimony.*
- (To an objection posed to extrinsic evidence)
  - (Where the witness with the alleged bias, prejudice, interest, or improper motive has not already testified) *The witness has been listed as a witness by my opponent and I offer this evidence conditionally to avoid recalling the witness presently on the stand at a later time.*
  - (Where the witness with the alleged bias, prejudice, interest, or improper motive has already testified) *I confronted* (insert name of witness) *with his or her* (bias, prejudice, interest, or improper motive) *during cross-examination when I asked* (insert question), *and he or she denied it.*

Cross-Reference to Illinois Law

725 ILCS 125/6; 735 ILCS 5/8-101 (interest of witness may be shown for purpose of affecting credibility); People v. Timmons, 114 Ill. App. 3d 861, 449 N.E.2d 1366 (1983) (refusal to talk to counsel showing bias); People v. Triplett, 108 Ill. 2d 453, 485 N.E.2d 9 (1985) (showing state's witness has been arrested, charged, or convicted; but evidence purporting to show bias may be excluded if it is remote or uncertain); People v. Woolridge, 91 Ill. App. 3d 298, 414 N.E.2d 814 (1980)

(confrontation of witness first is a prerequisite to admissibility of extrinsic evidence of bias). See EDWARD W. CLEARY & MICHAEL H. GRAHAM, HANDBOOK OF ILLINOIS EVIDENCE § 607.7 (6th ed. 1994).

Explanation

Bias, prejudice, interest, and improper motive are particularly fertile areas for impeachment and are probably the most typical areas of impeachment with most witnesses. They all depend on the relationship of the witness with one of the parties or the subject of the litigation. Illinois law requires that where extrinsic evidence of the bias is offered the proponent must show that she confronted the witness who is being impeached with the fact of the bias, whereupon the witness denied the fact.

Impeachment: Character Evidence

Objections

- *I object. The character witness has insufficient knowledge of the witness's character to give an opinion.*
- *I object. The character witness has insufficient knowledge of the witness's reputation for dishonesty to report that opinion to the court.*

Response

- *A sufficient foundation has been laid to demonstrate the character witness's sufficient familiarity with:*
  - *the witness's character for dishonesty, or*
  - *the witness's reputation for honesty in the community.*

Cross-Reference to Illinois Law

People v. Nash, 36 Ill. 2d 275, 222 N.E.2d 473 (1966) (general rule); People v. Hermens, 5 Ill. 2d 277, 125 N.E.2d 500 (1955). See EDWARD W. CLEARY & MICHAEL H. GRAHAM, HANDBOOK OF ILLINOIS EVIDENCE §§ 608.1, 608.2, 608.4 (6th ed. 1994).

Explanation

A witness may be impeached by testimony that the witness has bad character for honesty. Once a witness has been impeached by evidence of dishonest character, such witness may be rehabilitated by the calling of a character witness who will testify as to the witness's character for honesty or truthfulness by way of reputation evidence. Note that under Illinois law the reputation witness cannot be cross-examined about specific instances of conduct on the part of the principal witness (People v. Hermens, *supra*). Federal Rule of Evidence 608(a) permits this kind of cross-examination.

Impeachment: Learned Treatises

Objection

- *I object. This is improper impeachment.*

Response

- *This statement is admissible to impeach the expert witness as a statement contained in a learned treatise.*
  - *I have called the statement to the attention of the expert,* and
  - *the statement is contained in a treatise or periodical written for professional colleagues,*
  - *which has been established as a reliable authority by the testimony or admission of the expert witness, by other expert testimony, or by judicial notice.*

Cross-Reference to Illinois Law

Darling v. Charleston Community Memorial Hospital, 33 Ill. 2d 326, 211 N.E.2d 253 (1965). See EDWARD W. CLEARY & MICHAEL H. GRAHAM, HANDBOOK OF ILLINOIS EVIDENCE § 705.2 (6th ed. 1994).

Explanation

A learned treatise is a book or article established as a reliable authority on a matter, ordinarily the subject of expert opinion, which is called to the attention of an expert witness on cross-examination. A foundation for the learned treatise may be laid through the expert who is on the stand, through some other expert, or through the taking of judicial notice by the trial judge of the learned nature of the writing. Under Illinois law learned treatises are admissible for impeachment purposes only. They are not substantive evidence. Federal Rule of Evidence 803(18) creates a hearsay exception for learned treatises.

Impeachment: Extrinsic Evidence
(The Collateral Evidence Rule)

Objection

- *I object. This evidence is collateral.*

Response

- *The evidence is non-collateral and is therefore proper extrinsic evidence of impeachment.*

Cross-Reference to Illinois Law

People v. Thomas, 217 Ill. App. 3d 698, 577 N.E.2d 831 (1991) (definition of non-collateral); People v. Gonzalez, 104 Ill. 2d 332, 472 N.E.2d 417 (1984) (bias is non-collateral); People v. Hallbeck, 277 Ill. App. 3d 59, 590 N.E.2d 971 (1992) (prior inconsistent statement—need to confront first); People v. Pfanschmidt, 262 Ill. 411, 104 N.E. 804 (1914) (contradiction must be non-collateral); People v. Montgomery, 47 Ill. 2d 510, 268 N.E.2d 695 (1971) (impeachment by showing prior conviction). See Impeachment: Prior Convictions, p. 143, *infra*. See EDWARD W. CLEARY & MICHAEL H. GRAHAM, HANDBOOK OF ILLINOIS EVIDENCE § 607.2 (6th ed. 1994).

Explanation

Impeachment evidence offered outside of (extrinsic to) the cross-examination of the witness to be impeached is called extrinsic evidence. Extrinsic evidence is thus defined by timing—at a time other than during cross. In order to be admissible, extrinsic evidence must be non-collateral. A matter is non-collateral if it is relevant for any purpose other than mere contradiction of the witness (Cleary and Graham, *supra*, citing People v. Thomas). Certain matters are categorically non-collateral: bias, prior convictions, competency of an expert witness. Impeachment by prior inconsistent statement and by contradiction are governed, on a case-by-case basis, by the basic definition of non-collateral: if relevant for some purpose other than the mere contradiction.

An additional foundation prerequisite applies to introduction of extrinsic evidence of bias and of a prior inconsistent statement. The proponent must first confront the witness with the facts which show bias or the statement during cross-examination. (People v. Hallberg, *supra*; see Impeachment: Bias Prejudice, Interest, and Improper Motive, p. 130, *supra*).

Impeachment: Impeachment of One's Own Witness

Objection

- *I object. Counsel is impeaching her own witness.*

Response

- *Under Supreme Court Rule 238 (433 in criminal cases) the credibility of a witness may be attacked by any party, including the party calling the witness.*

Cross-Reference to Illinois Law

Supreme Court Rule 238(a), 433; People v. Chitwood, 36 Ill. App. 3d 1017, 344 N.E.2d 611 (1976) (definition of surprise and affirmative damage); People v. Cruz, 162 Ill. 2d 314, 643 N.E.2d 636 (1994) (requirement of surprise and affirmative damage). See EDWARD W. CLEARY & MICHAEL H. GRAHAM, HANDBOOK OF ILLINOIS EVIDENCE § 607.4 (6th ed. 1994).

Explanation

By Supreme Court rule any party may attack the credibility of a witness, including the party who called the witness. A party may not call a witness just to impeach her. In People v. Cruz, *supra*, the court held that in order to impeach a witness whom one has called with prior inconsistent statements which are not admissible as substantive evidence (see Hearsay: Non-Hearsay Prior Statements: Prior Inconsistent Statements in a Criminal Case, p. 71, *supra*), the examiner must show "surprise and affirmative damage." The meaning of surprise is self-evident; affirmative damage is obscure. In People v. Chitwood, *supra*, the court said that affirmative damage means more than that the witness's answer is disappointing to the examiner, by failing to include a fact which the examiner was expecting. To justify impeachment, the answer must contradict an aspect of the examiner's case. It's the difference between "The defendant didn't do it" and "I don't remember saying the defendant did it."

Impeachment: Memory and Perception

Objection

- *I object. The question seeks to elicit irrelevant information; the question involves improper impeachment.*

Response

- *The question calls for an answer that will show the witness's inability to remember the events about which testimony has been given or his inability to perceive. This is proper cross-examination.*

Cross-Reference to Illinois Law

See EDWARD W. CLEARY & MICHAEL H. GRAHAM, HANDBOOK OF ILLINOIS EVIDENCE § 607.1 (6th ed. 1994).

Explanation

An obvious corollary to the requirement that a witness must be able to observe, record, recollect, and recount is the relevance of an attack on cross-examination which is designed to show that the witness's memory is faulty, and that her perception is inaccurate.

Impeachment: Prior Convictions

Objection

- *I object. The proffered conviction is improper impeachment.*

Response

- *The proffered conviction is admissible under the rule of People v. Montgomery:*
  - *the conviction is for a crime punishable by death or imprisonment for more than one year under the law under which the witness was convicted, or*
  - *the conviction is for a crime which involves dishonesty or false statement,* and
  - *the probative value of the conviction is not substantially outweighed by the danger of unfair prejudice,* and
  - *less than 10 years have elapsed since the date of conviction (or release of the witness from confinement, whichever date is later).*

Cross-Reference to Illinois Law

People v. Montgomery, 471 Ill. 2d 510, 268 N.E.2d 695 (1971); People v. Williams, 173 Ill.

2d 48, 670 N.E.2d 638 (1996) ("Williams II"); 735 ILCS 5/8-101 (method of proof—civil); People v. Roche, 389 Ill. 361, 59 N.E.2d 866 (1945) (method of proof—criminal—witness other than accused); People v. Madison, 56 Ill. 2d 476, 309 N.E.2d 11 (1974) (method of proof—criminal—the accused).

Explanation

Illinois law differs markedly from Federal Rule of Evidence 609. There is no distinction, in terms of the criteria for admissibility, between the accused in a criminal case and witnesses and parties generally. In addition, all convictions are balanced, with the burden on the person opposing admissibility to show that the danger of unfair prejudice <u>substantially</u> outweighs probative value. Convictions older than 10 years are excluded. (The 10 years is calculated by excluding time spent in custody.)

There is one distinction between the criminal accused and other witnesses: with witnesses generally the conviction may be established on cross-examination of the witness himself, or in rebuttal in other forms, such as a certified copy of the record of conviction (People v. Roche, *supra*). With the accused, however, unless he addresses the conviction himself on direct examination, the <u>only</u> method of proof is by certified copy offered in rebuttal (People v. Madison, *supra*). The Illinois

Supreme Court in "Williams II," *supra*, reaffirmed the Montgomery rule, emphasizing that convictions for all crimes must be balanced and that admissibility is not limited to crimes of dishonesty or false statement.

Impeachment:
Prior Inconsistent Statements

Objection

- *I object. The proffered statement is not inconsistent with the witness's testimony and is irrelevant.*

Response

- *The statement is inconsistent with the witness's testimony, and I have a good faith basis for asking the question.*

Cross-Reference to Illinois Law

People v. Flores, 128 Ill. 2d 66, 538 N.E.2d 481 (1989) (defining inconsistency); People v. Olinger, 112 Ill. 2d 324, 493 N.E.2d 579 (1986) (good faith basis means ability to prove up if denied). For offering extrinsic evidence of the prior statement, when denied, see Impeachment: Extrinsic Evidence (The Collateral Evidence Rule), p. 137, *supra*. See EDWARD W. CLEARY & MICHAEL H. GRAHAM, HANDBOOK OF ILLINOIS EVIDENCE § 613.1–613.3 (6th ed. 1994).

Explanation

Prior inconsistent statements of a witness discredit precisely because of the inconsistency. They are not hearsay because what is relevant in this instance is the inconsistency, not the truth or falsity of the statement. Yet "inconsistent" is defined loosely; it includes, in addition to directly contradictory statements, those which have a reasonable tendency to discredit the witness's testimony (People v. Flores, *supra*).

The examiner needs a good faith basis, however, to confront the witness with a question about the prior statement. Good faith means ability to prove that the statement was made if it is denied (People v. Olinger, *supra*). If the statement is denied and extrinsic evidence of it is offered, the statement must be non-collateral, i.e., it must relate to something which is relevant apart from the contradiction.

Impeachment: Specific Instances of Misconduct

Objection

- *I object. Evidence of specific instances of misconduct is an impermissible form of impeachment.*

Response

- *(There is no response.)*

Cross-Reference to Illinois Law

People v. Celmars, 332 Ill. 113, 163 N.E. 421 (1928) (specific instances of misconduct not permitted). See EDWARD W. CLEARY & MICHAEL H. GRAHAM, HANDBOOK OF ILLINOIS EVIDENCE § 608.5 (6th ed. 1994).

Explanation

Illinois law has a long-standing, strict prohibition against evidence of the witness's own acts of misconduct to impeach. Federal Rule of Evidence 608(b) permits such impeachment so long as the examiner has a good faith basis in believing the misconduct occurred, and the misconduct relates to honesty.

Insurance Against Liability

Objection

- *I object. The proponent is offering evidence of liability insurance on the issue of negligence or other wrongful conduct. I move for a mistrial.*

Response

- *This evidence of liability insurance is not offered on the issue of negligence, but to show:*
  - *ownership,*
  - *agency,*
  - *control,*
  - *bias, or*
  - *some purpose other than liability.*

Cross-Reference to Illinois Law

Pagano v. Leisner, 5 Ill. App. 2d 223, 125 N.E.2d 301 (1955) (general rule); Williams v. Consumers Co., 352 Ill. 51, 185 N.E. 217 (1933) (mistrial is not automatic). See EDWARD W. CLEARY & MICHAEL H. GRAHAM, HANDBOOK OF ILLINOIS EVIDENCE § 411.1 (6th ed. 1994).

Explanation

Contrary to common belief, the mere mention of the defendant's being insured against liability is not necessarily inadmissible, nor need it lead to a mistrial. Evidence of insurance generally is not admissible only on the issues of liability and the ability of a party to pay damages, but may be admissible for any other relevant purpose.

Judicial Notice

Objection

- *I object to the court judicially noticing* (insert fact offered) *in that*
  - *it is not generally known in this jurisdiction,* and/or
  - *it is not so capable of verification as to be beyond reasonable controversy.*

Response

- *Judicial notice of* (insert fact offered) *is appropriate because:*
  - *the fact is generally known* or
  - *it is capable of verification so as to be beyond reasonable controversy.*

Cross-Reference to Illinois Law

Owens v. Green, 400 Ill. 380, 81 N.E.2d 149 (1948)(matters generally known); Murray v. Edgar, 103 Ill. 2d 384, 469 N.E.2d 1085 (1984) (matters capable of verification); Nicketta v. National Tea Co., 338 Ill. App. 159, 87 N.E.2d 30 (1949) (procedure); People v. Speight, 222 Ill. App. 3d 766, 584 N.E.2d 392 (1991) (sua sponte judicial notice).

Explanation

The party seeking judicial notice must supply the court with sufficient information to enable the court to take judicial notice. The court also may judicially notice an appropriate fact on its own motion. The opposing party has the right to be heard concerning the propriety of judicial notice. Once the court takes judicial notice, however, the proponent is prohibited from contesting the fact which the court has noticed.

Lay Opinion Evidence

Objections

- *I object. The question calls for an opinion.*
- *I move to strike the answer because it is stated in the form of opinion.*

Response

- *This is permissible opinion from a lay witness because it is rationally based on the perception of the witness and would help the trier of fact to understand the witness's testimony and determine a fact in issue in this lawsuit.*

Cross-Reference to Illinois Law

Freeding-Skokie Rolloff Service v. Hamilton, 108 Ill. 2d 217, 483 N.E.2d 524 (1985) (lay opinion admissible when helpful to a clear understanding of witness's testimony or a determination of a fact in issue); Scheibel v. Groesteka, 183 Ill. App. 3d 120, 538 N.E.2d 1236 (1989) (Illinois courts rely on Fed. R. Evid. 701); People v. Burton, 6 Ill. App. 3d 879, 286 N.E.2d 792 (1972) (foundation). See EDWARD W. CLEARY & MICHAEL H. GRAHAM, HANDBOOK OF ILLINOIS EVIDENCE § 701.1–701.8 (6th ed. 1994).

Explanation

Lay opinion is generally allowed where its admission makes the jury's fact-finding easier and more accurate. A typical admissible lay opinion occurs where a witness provides an inference to the jury which takes the place of describing a series of perceptions which in common experience add up to a rather ordinary inference or characterization (e.g., testimony that someone looked happy, sad, confused, angry, etc.). The opinion must be one that a lay person could normally form from observed facts.

Leading Questions

Objection

- *I object to the question as leading.*

Responses

- *The question does not suggest the answer to the witness,* or
- *Leading questions are permitted:*
  - *on preliminary matters,* or
  - *because the witness is hostile, is an adverse party, or is identified with an adverse party,* or
  - *the witness is a child or an adult with a communication problem,* or
  - *the witness's recollection is exhausted,* or
  - *this is redirect examination.*

Cross-Reference to Illinois Law

Cannon v. People, 141 Ill. 270, 30 N.E. 1027 (1892) (preliminary matters); Supreme Court Rule 238(b) (witness who is hostile, unwilling, or frightened); 735 ILCS 5/2-1102 (adverse witness); People v. Luigs, 96 Ill. App. 3d 700, 421 N.E.2d 961 (1981) (child witness); Reed v. Northwestern Publishing

Co., 124 Ill. 2d 495, 530 N.E.2d 474 (1988) (refreshing recollection); Cruz v. Gulf M. & O. Ry., 7 Ill. App. 2d 209, 129 N.E.2d 272 (1955) (redirect examination). See EDWARD W. CLEARY & MICHAEL H. GRAHAM, HANDBOOK OF ILLINOIS EVIDENCE § 611.9 (6th ed. 1994).

Explanation

A leading question is one which suggests the desired answer to the witness so that it puts the desired answer in the witness's mouth or is one which makes it unclear as to whether the witness or the lawyer is testifying. The rule against leading is honored more in the breach than in the observance because leading is permitted in a variety of situations, as indicated above. Moreover, while a leading objection is the opponent's objection, leading questions pose a serious problem for the examiner because, in leading on material matters, she is preventing the witness from establishing his credibility.

Misquoting the Witness

Objection

- *I object. Counsel is misquoting the witness. The witness has testified to* (insert substance of witness's testimony).

Response

- *The witness previously testified to* (insert substance of witness's testimony).

Cross-Reference to Illinois Law

Briggs v. People, 219 Ill. 330, 76 N.E. 499 (1905). See EDWARD W. CLEARY & MICHAEL H. GRAHAM, HANDBOOK OF ILLINOIS EVIDENCE § 611.22 (6th ed. 1994).

Explanation

This objection is designed to prevent opposing counsel from shading the testimony of the witness as it had previously been rendered. The objection can serve as a reminder to the witness to listen carefully to opposing counsel's questions before answering.

Narratives

Objections

- *I object. The question calls for a narrative response.*
- *I object. The witness is testifying in the form of a narrative.*

Response

- *The witness is testifying to relevant and admissible matters.*

Cross-Reference to Illinois Law

Franklin v. Randolph, 130 Ill. App. 2d 801, 267 N.E.2d 337 (1971). ("Tell us everything that was said that night"); Kozlowski v. City of Chicago, 113 Ill. App. 513 (1904) ("What has been the effect of the injury on your health?"). See EDWARD W. CLEARY & MICHAEL H. GRAHAM, HANDBOOK OF ILLINOIS EVIDENCE § 611.20 (6th ed. 1994).

Explanation

Questions which call for narrative answers, and narrative answers themselves, prevent the opponent from making timely objection. In the normal give and take of pointed, specific question and answer, the question alerts the opponent to objectionable material. Counsel should object promptly to a question which calls for a narrative response, so as to prevent inadmissible evidence from being mentioned. Often, a motion to strike in such a situation may only worsen things by emphasizing the inadmissible evidence, so counsel must act promptly to prevent the narrative from unfolding.

Non-Responsive Answers

Objection

- *I move to strike the answer of the witness as non-responsive.*

Response

- *The answer of the witness is responsive to the question. The question put to the witness was* (insert the form of the question).

Cross-Reference to Illinois Law

Math v. Chicago City Ry., 243 Ill. 114, 90 N.E. 235 (1909) (non-responsive answers should be stricken); Hester v. Goldsbury, 64 Ill. App. 2d 66, 212 N.E.2d 316 (1965) (objection is the examiner's to make, not the opponent's). See EDWARD W. CLEARY & MICHAEL H. GRAHAM, HANDBOOK OF ILLINOIS EVIDENCE § 611.19 (6th ed. 1994).

Explanation

The objection of non-responsiveness belongs only to questioning counsel. Answers which exceed the scope of the question may be the subject of a motion to strike by opposing counsel on specific substantive grounds. Opposing counsel may also object to the testimony of a witness as testimony in a narrative form (see Narratives, p. 158, *supra*).

Objections

Objection

(See specific objections under appropriate captions in this text for forms of objections.)

Responses

(See specific responses under appropriate captions in this text for forms of responses.)

Cross-Reference to Illinois Law

People v. Carlson, 79 Ill. 2d 564, 404 N.E.2d (1980) (waiver if no objection). See EDWARD W. CLEARY & MICHAEL H. GRAHAM, HANDBOOK OF ILLINOIS EVIDENCE § 103.1–103.4 (6th ed. 1994).

Explanation

Generally, failure to object waives appellate consideration of any error in the admission of evidence at trial. Objections must state the specific ground for exclusion of evidence unless the ground for objection is obvious. Objections must be timely in that they must be stated as soon as the objectionable nature of the question or answer becomes apparent.

Offers of Proof

Forms of the Offer

- Ask the witness to state for the record, outside the hearing of the jury, what the witness's testimony would have been if the judge had not excluded it; or

- A statement by the counsel who attempted to offer the witness's statement, which provides the substance of what the witness's testimony would have been, but for the adverse ruling; or

- A prepared written statement of the witness's testimony which would have been given, but for the adverse ruling.

Cross-Reference to Illinois Law

People v. Keen, 206 Ill. App. 3d 940, 564 N.E.2d 1314 (1990) (offer of proof required when it is not clear what witness would say, what is the basis for her testimony, or what the purpose of the evidence is); People v. Andrews, 146 Ill. 2d 413, 588 N.E.2d 1126 (1992) (failure to make offer of proof precludes raising issue on appeal); Hall v. Northwestern University Medical Clinics, 152 Ill. App. 3d 716, 504 N.E.2d 1358 (1993) (method—question and answer); People v. Lynch, 104 Ill. 2d 194, 470 N.E.2d 1018 (1984) (error to refuse counsel's request to make an offer of proof). See EDWARD W. CLEARY & MICHAEL H. GRAHAM, HANDBOOK OF ILLINOIS EVIDENCE § 103.7 (6th ed. 1994).

Explanation

The offer of proof is made outside the presence of the jury, either by counsel stating what the testimony would be or by counsel examining the witness. The offer must be made at the time of the sustaining of an objection or it will be waived. The purpose of the rule is to give the trial judge the best opportunity to make the proper ruling. Given the waiver which attaches to failure to make an offer of proof counsel must aggressively, though courteously, seek permission to make an offer. Refusal to permit an offer can be error (People v. Lynch, *supra*).

Original Document Rule
(Best Evidence Rule)

Objection

- *I object. The proffered testimony (or exhibit) is secondary evidence of the contents of a writing.*

Responses

- *The original is not required because I am not attempting to prove a fact or event by using a writing. The testimony (or exhibit) is offered to prove* (state reason), or

- *I am trying to prove a fact or event by using the contents of a writing, and although I do not have the original,*

- *The original's absence has been sufficiently accounted for and the secondary evidence is admissible because:*
  - *the original has been shown to have been lost or destroyed,* or
  - *the original cannot be obtained by any available judicial process or procedure,* or
  - *the original is in the possession of an opposing party against whom the contents are offered, that party has failed to produce it, and that party has been put on notice, by pleadings or*

> *otherwise, that the contents would be the subject of proof at trial,* or
- *The matter is collateral.*

Cross-Reference to Illinois Law

Larson v. Commonwealth Edison Co., 33 Ill. 2d 316, 211 N.E.2d 247 (1965) (general rule); People v. Spencer, 264 Ill. 124, 106 N.E. 219 (1914) (applies only when contents of a writing are sought to be proved); People v. Wells, 380 Ill. 347, 44 N.E.2d 32 (1942) (duplicates not generally equated with original); 735 ILCS 5/8-401, 725 ILCS 5/115-5(b) (providing for admissibility of duplicates, in certain circumstances, in civil and criminal cases). See also Competence to Testify: The Dead Man's Act, p. 33, *supra*); 735 ILCS 5/8-1202 (certified copy of judicial proceedings); 735 ILCS 5/8-1206 (duplicates of court, municipal, and private court records admissible); Supreme Court Rule 216(a) (duplicate copies of public records). See EDWARD W. CLEARY & MICHAEL H. GRAHAM, HANDBOOK OF ILLINOIS EVIDENCE §§ 1001–1008 (6th ed. 1994).

Explanation

The labyrinthine scheme of the original writing rule applies only when the proponent seeks to prove a fact or event by using a writing. Typical documents that fall within the rule are written contracts, leases, or wills when the lawsuit is about the existence or interpretation of those documents. On the other hand, for example, a party may prove a conversation, or a confession, by resort to oral testimony, even if the conversation or confession has been written or recorded. If the proponent seeks to prove the conversation or confession <u>by referring to the writing or recording</u>, however, then she needs to offer the original or account for her failure to produce it.

Unlike Federal Rule of Evidence 1003, Illinois common law does not treat duplicates generally as equivalent to an original. Several statutory provisions, *supra*, make duplicates admissible in certain circumstances.

Payment of Medical and Similar Expenses

Objection

- *I object. This evidence is inadmissible as an offer to pay medical expenses.*

Response

- *This statement is admissible because it is not offered on the issue of liability.*

Cross-Reference to Illinois Law

735 ILCS 5/8-1901 (offer to pay or payment "shall not be construed as an admission of liability"). See EDWARD W. CLEARY & MICHAEL H. GRAHAM, HANDBOOK OF ILLINOIS EVIDENCE § 409.1 (6th ed. 1994).

Explanation

Evidence of offers to pay medical and similar expenses, or payments of the same, are excluded only on the issue of liability and can be offered for any other relevant purpose.

Presumptions

Form of Motion

- *I move for a directed verdict on* (the fact presumed) *because my opponent failed to come forward with sufficient evidence to rebut it.*

Response

- *A directed verdict is inappropriate because we have produced sufficient evidence to rebut the presumption such that a reasonable juror could find for my client on this fact.*

Cross-Reference to Illinois Law

(Franciscan Sisters Health Care Corp. v. Dean, 95 Ill. 2d 452, 448 N.E.2d 872 (1983) (Illinois generally follows "bursting bubble" theory of presumptions; in some instances, however, "clear and convincing evidence" may be necessary to rebut). See EDWARD W. CLEARY & MICHAEL H. GRAHAM, HANDBOOK OF ILLINOIS EVIDENCE § 802.1–802.11 (6th ed. 1994).

Explanation

A presumption is a device by which proof of one fact automatically constitutes proof of another fact.

Presumptions are embodied in statutes or in jury instructions in the following form: "If you find X you must find Y" or "Proof of X establishes Y." Under Illinois law a presumption forces the opponent to come forward with sufficient evidence to rebut or meet the presumed fact. The presumption does not, however, shift the burden of proof. Sufficient evidence ordinarily means evidence from which a jury could find the non-existence of the presumed fact by a preponderance of the evidence. In some cases, however, Illinois law, while not shifting the burden of proof, does require the opponent to offer clear and convincing evidence of the non-existence of the presumed fact. This higher burden of production appears limited to presumptions based upon significant social policies, such as the lawyer's fiduciary duty to her client, at issue in the Franciscan Sisters case, *supra*.

Privileges

Objection

- *I object to the admission of this evidence on the ground that it is privileged pursuant to* (state the particular form of privilege).

Response

- *This evidence is admissible because:*
  - *it does not fall within the privilege,* or
  - *if privileged, such privilege has been waived.*

Cross-Reference to Illinois Law

735 ILCS 5/8-802 (physician-patient); 740 ILCS 110/10 (psychiatrist-patient in Mental Health and Developmental Disabilities Act); 725 ILCS 5/104-14 (defendant's statements to court-appointed psychiatrist, appointed to determine competency to stand trial); 735 ILCS 5/8-802.1 (statements by rape victim to rape-crisis counselor); 735 ILCS 5/8-802.2 (statements made by victims of violent crime to counselor of a victim aid organization); 735 ILCS 5/8-803 (communications to member of the clergy); 735 ILCS 5/8-801 (husband-wife); 225 ILCS 450/27 (public accountant privilege); 735 ILCS 5/8-901–909 (reporter's privilege); 225 ILCS 20/16 (social worker privilege); but note 735 ILCS

5/2-1003 (requires <u>waiver</u> of privilege for communications between party and health care provider when party claims bodily injury or disease or mental health injury or disease); People v. Adam, 51 Ill. 2d 46, 289 N.E.2d 205 (1972) (attorney-client). See EDWARD W. CLEARY & MICHAEL H. GRAHAM, HANDBOOK OF ILLINOIS EVIDENCE §§ 503.1–503.9, 505.1–505.11 (6th ed. 1994).

Explanation

The three most commonly encountered privileged communications in Illinois courts are the attorney-client privilege, the privileges applicable to spouses, and the physician-patient privilege. The statutory expansion of privileges in Illinois requires counsel as part of her trial preparation to assess her proof in light of this welter of exclusionary rules.

Refreshing Present Recollection

Objections

- *I object to the attempt to refresh the witness's recollection in the absence of a demonstrated failure of memory.*
- *I object to the witness's reading from the exhibit used to refresh his or her recollection because it is not in evidence and because it is hearsay.*

Response

- *The witness has shown a failure of memory and I am attempting to refresh his or her recollection.*

Cross-Reference to Illinois Law

People v. Olson, 59 Ill. App. 3d 643, 375 N.E.2d 533 (1978) (anything can be used to refresh recollection); Northern Illinois Gas Co. v. Vincent DiVito Construction, 214 Ill. App. 3d 203, 573 N.E.2d 243 (1991) (need not be witness's own memorandum); People v. Black, 84 Ill. App. 3d 1050, 406 N.E.2d 23 (1980) (court has considerable discretion in deciding whether witness has had recollection refreshed or is merely reading from document). See EDWARD W. CLEARY & MICHAEL H. GRAHAM, HANDBOOK OF ILLINOIS EVIDENCE § 612.1 (6th ed. 1994).

Explanation

The steps in refreshing a witness's memory are as follows:

(1) Establish the witness's failure of memory (full or partial).
(2) Mark the refreshing document for identification.
(3) Show the witness the refreshing document and ask the witness to read it silently.
(4) Ask if the witness has read it.
(5) Ask if the witness's memory is refreshed with respect to the forgotten fact.
(6) Take the refreshing exhibit from the witness.
(7) Re-ask the question which drew the original failure of memory.

Relevance: Generally

Objections

- *I object on the ground that the question calls for an irrelevant answer.*
- *I move to strike the answer as irrelevant.*

Response

- *The evidence is relevant because it has some tendency to make more likely a fact which is material to either a claim or defense in the lawsuit or bears on the weight or credibility of the evidence.*

Cross-Reference to Illinois Law

People v. Boclair, 129 Ill. 2d 458, 544 N.E.2d 715 (1989) (court adopts Fed. R. Evid. 401 definition of relevance). See EDWARD W. CLEARY & MICHAEL H. GRAHAM, HANDBOOK OF ILLINOIS EVIDENCE § 401.1 (6th ed. 1994).

Explanation

Often, the terms "relevance" and "materiality" are used interchangeably. This is incorrect. Materiality has a more precise meaning than relevance and can be seen as being a term which is within the meaning of relevance. Materiality is the relationship between the proposition for which the evidence is offered and the issues in the case. If the evidence is offered to prove a proposition which is not a matter in issue, the evidence is said to be immaterial. Relevancy includes both the test of materiality and something more. Relevancy is the tendency of the evidence in question to establish a material proposition.

Relevance: Conditional Relevance
(and Conditional Admissibility)

Objection

- *I object. The evidence is relevant only if* (insert fact or facts) *are true. There has been no evidence offered to prove those facts (or the evidence which has been offered is insufficient to support a finding that the facts are true).*

Responses

- *I will show the relevance of the proffered evidence by proof of the following additional facts through the testimony of* (insert name of witness).

- *The relevance of the conditionally admitted facts has been shown through the evidence given in the testimony of* (insert name of witness).

Cross-Reference to Illinois Law

Marvel Eng. Co. v. Commercial Union Insurance Co., 118 Ill. App. 3d 844, 455 N.E.2d 545 (1983) (Illinois law is same as Fed. R. Evid. 104(b), adopting concept of conditional relevance). See EDWARD

W. Cleary & Michael H. Graham, Handbook of Illinois Evidence § 104.1 (6th ed. 1994).

Explanation

Conditional relevance and conditional admissibility refer to two different ideas. Conditional admissibility describes a sequence of proof; conditional relevance describes the analytical role the judge should play in deciding certain admissibility questions.

In a case of conditional admissibility the proponent asks the court to admit testimony or an exhibit into evidence even though the complete foundation has not been established. The court may accept such evidence "conditionally," i.e., on the condition that the proponent prove up the missing parts of the foundation, which parts could be any aspect of foundation, e.g., a showing of authentication, a portion of a hearsay exception foundation, or an aspect of the original writing rule requirements. If counsel does not prove up the foundation, the evidence which has been admitted conditionally will be stricken.

Conditional relevance, on the other hand, refers to the role the judge is to play in deciding certain admissibility questions. The very requirement of evidentiary foundation means, on admissibility issues, the judge is always playing some role in deciding whether certain foundation or preliminary facts are true. Ordinarily the judge decides whether she is herself convinced, usually by a preponderance, that the foundation or preliminary facts exist. In some instances, however, the law desires the judge to take a less active role in deciding whether foundation facts exist. In these instances the only issue is whether certain facts are true or not; there is no overlay of policy or interpretation. As to these facts the jury is in as good a position as the judge to decide whether the facts are true. To require that the judge be persuaded in this instance threatens to transform a jury trial into a bench trial. These instances are therefore referred to as matters of conditional relevance. As to them the judge is only to screen the evidence, that is, to ask "could a jury find that these facts exist?" Whether a matter involves only conditional relevance, or rather the application of the myriad substantive rules of evidence, with their policy and interpretative overlay, is often difficult to answer. A reasonable working definition is: an issue should be treated as a question of conditional relevance when the jurors can ignore the proffered evidence if they find the preliminary or foundation facts don't exist. If, however, the proffered evidence would still influence the jury even if the foundation were lacking—like a confession in a criminal case challenged on voluntariness grounds—then the judge should take an active role and decide for himself whether the preliminary facts exist. The Illinois Appellate Court accepted the concept of conditional relevance in Marvel Engineering, *supra*.

Relevance: Exclusion of Relevant Evidence on Grounds of Prejudice, Confusion, or Waste of Time

Objections

- *I object on the ground that this evidence is inadmissible because its probative value is substantially outweighed by the prejudicial effect of the evidence.*
- *The introduction of this evidence will confuse the issue before the jury.*
- *The evidence is merely cumulative.*

Response

- *The evidence is admissible because it is logically relevant and:*
  - *its probative value is not substantially outweighed by the danger of unfair prejudice, or*
  - *any potential confusion of issues is easily cured by an instruction by the court, or*
  - *the evidence is corroborative of an issue central to the case.*

Cross-Reference to Illinois Law

People v. Chambers, 179 Ill. App. 3d 565, 534 N.E.2d 554 (1989) (general balancing rule); People v. Sutherland, 155 Ill. 2d 1, 610 N.E.2d 1 (1992) (prejudice); Simmons v. City of Chicago, 243 Ill. App. 3d 552, 611 N.E.2d 1296 (1993) (cumulative evidence); People v. Schulz, 154 Ill. App. 3d 358, 506 N.E.2d 1343 (1987) (confusion of issues). See EDWARD W. CLEARY & MICHAEL H. GRAHAM, HANDBOOK OF ILLINOIS EVIDENCE § 403.1 (6th ed. 1994).

Explanation

The common law balancing test (articulated in Federal Rule of Evidence 403) is tilted heavily in favor of the admissibility of logically relevant evidence or evidence with probative value, in that the prejudice must substantially outweigh the probative value in order to require exclusion.

Relevance: Limited Admissibility

Objections

- *I object. The question calls for irrelevant information on the issue* (insert the issue).

- *I object. I move the court instruct the jury that the answer is irrelevant and inadmissible on the issue* (insert the issue) *and I request a limiting instruction.*

- *I object. The question calls for irrelevant information as against my client.*

- *I object. I move the court instruct the jury the answer is irrelevant and inadmissible as to my client and I request a limiting instruction.*

Responses

- *The evidence offered is relevant and admissible for all purposes and a limiting instruction is inappropriate.*

- *The evidence is relevant and admissible against all parties and a limiting instruction is inappropriate.*

Cross-Reference to Illinois Law

People v. Taylor, 66 Ill. App. 3d 907, 384 N.E.2d 558 (1978) (general rule supporting limiting instruction); People v. Gacho, 122 Ill. 2d 221, 522 N.E.2d 1146 (1988) (court is not under a duty to issue a limiting instruction sua sponte). See EDWARD W. CLEARY & MICHAEL H. GRAHAM, HANDBOOK OF ILLINOIS EVIDENCE § 105 (6th ed. 1994).

Explanation

If opposing counsel seeks limitation of the evidence to its admissible purposes, she must request a limiting instruction by the judge. The judge is not required to give a limiting instruction sua sponte (People v. Gacho, *supra*). A corollary of this principle is that the judge will not give a limiting instruction over counsel's objection. Counsel should carefully assess the desirability of a limiting instruction, since such an instruction often only highlights the proscribed use for the jury. Often, therefore, the best strategy is to live with the evidence and deal with the problem of its meaning in closing argument.

Relevance:
Rule of Completeness

Objections

- *I object to the admissibility of the proffered writing (or recording) unless other portions of the writing (or recording) are also admitted. These other portions are necessary to explain or to put in context the proffered writing (or recording).*

- *I object to the admissibility of the proffered writing (or recording) unless other related writings (or recordings) are also admitted. These other writings (or recordings) are necessary to explain (or to put in context) the proffered writing (or recording).*

Response

- *The proffered statement (or recording) does not need explanation or context. Other portions of the statement (or recording), or additional writings (or recordings), are not necessary to a fair understanding of the proffered statement (or recording).*

Cross-Reference to Illinois Law

Lawson v. G. D. Searle & Co., 64 Ill. 2d 543, 356 N.E.2d 779 (1976) (general rule); Supreme Court Rule 212(c) (requirement that where deposition is read or used opponent may read or use any other part which ought in fairness to be considered). See EDWARD W. CLEARY & MICHAEL H. GRAHAM, HANDBOOK OF ILLINOIS EVIDENCE § 106.1 (6th ed. 1994).

Explanation

The rule of completeness is essentially a rule of fairness. Because the appearance of unfairness can seriously damage the credibility of the proponent, the rule of completeness should be anticipated by proffering counsel and every effort should be made to fairly show the appropriate context in which an offered statement or recording was made.

Subsequent Remedial Measures

Objection

- *I object. This is evidence of a subsequent remedial measure.*

Responses

- *This evidence is not offered on the issue of negligence or culpable conduct, but is offered to show:*
  - *notice,*
  - *ownership,*
  - *control,*
  - *feasibility of precautionary measures, or*
  - *impeachment.*
- *My opponent has "opened the door" to this evidence by:*
  - *its pleadings* or
  - *the questioning of* (insert name of witness).

Cross-Reference to Illinois Law

Schaffner v. Chicago and N. W. Transportation Co., 129 Ill. 2d 1, 541 N.E.2d 643 (1989) (general rule); Davis v. International Harvester Co., 167 Ill. App. 3d 814, 521 N.E.2d 1282 (1988) (exclusionary rule applies in products liability cases). See EDWARD

W. CLEARY & MICHAEL H. GRAHAM, HANDBOOK OF ILLINOIS EVIDENCE § 407.1 (6th ed. 1994).

Explanation

The reason for the evidentiary prohibition against subsequent remedial measures is to create an incentive for correction of defective conditions. Such evidence is per se inadmissible only on the issues of negligence or culpable conduct.

Illinois law extends this exclusionary rule to products liability cases (Davis v. International Harvester Co., *supra*).

Illinois Compiled Statutes

Illinois Supreme Court Rules

Table of Contents

Illinois Compiled Statutes

§ 225 ILCS 20/16. Privileged Communications
and Exceptions 195

§ 225 ILCS 450/27. Confidential Information . 197

§ 305 ILCS 5/10-13.4. Proof of Records 198

§ 410 ILCS 535/1. Definitions 198

§ 725 ILCS 5/104-14. Use of Statements Made
During Examination or Treatment 200

§ 725 ILCS 5/115-5. Business Records as
Evidence 202

§ 725 ILCS 5/115-5.1. Coroner's Records as
Evidence 204

§ 725 ILCS 5/115-7. Prior Sexual Activity or
Reputation of Victim of Sexual Offense . . 205

§ 725 ILCS 5/115-7.3. Evidence in Certain
Cases 207

§ 725 ILCS 5/115.10. Certain Hearsay
Exceptions 209

§ 725 ILCS 5/115-10.1. Admissibility of Prior
Inconsistent Statements 212

§ 725 ILCS 5/115-10.2. Admissibility of Prior
Statements When Witness Refused to
Testify Despite a Court Order to Testify . . 213

§ 725 ILCS 5/115-13. Medical Records as
Evidence in Trial for Sexual Offense 215

§ 725 ILCS 5/115-14. Witness Competency . . 215

§ 725 ILCS 5/115-15. Laboratory Reports . . . 216

§ 735 ILCS 5/2-1002. [Repealed] 218

§ 735 ILCS 5/2-1102. Examination of Adverse
Party or Agent 218
§ 735 ILCS 5/8-101. Interested Witness 218
§ 735 ILCS 5/8-201. Dead Man's Act 219
§ 735 ILCS 5/8-401. Account Books and
Records 221
§ 735 ILCS 5/8-801. Husband and Wife 222
§ 735 ILCS 5/8-802. Healthcare Practitioner
and Patient 222
§ 735 ILCS 5/8-802.1. Confidentiality of Statements Made to Rape Crisis Personnel . . . 226
§ 735 ILCS 5/8-802.2. Confidentiality of Statements Made to Personnel Counseling
Victims of Violent Crimes 230
§ 735 ILCS 5/8-803. Clergy 231
§ 735 ILCS 5/8-901. Source of Information . . 232
§ 735 ILCS 5/8-902. Definitions 232
§ 735 ILCS 5/8-903. Application to Court . . . 232
§ 735 ILCS 5/8-904. Contents of Application . 233
§ 735 ILCS 5/8-905. Civil Proceeding 234
§ 735 ILCS 5/8-906. Consideration by Court . 234
§ 735 ILCS 5/8-907. Court's Findings 234
§ 735 ILCS 5/8-908. Privilege Continues
During Pendency of Appeal 235
§ 735 ILCS 5/8-909. Contempt 236
§ 735 ILCS 5/8-1202. Court Records 236
§ 735 ILCS 5/8-1203. Municipal Records . . . 236
§ 735 ILCS 5/8-1204. Corporate Records . . . 236
§ 735 ILCS 5/8-1205. Form of Certificate . . . 237
§ 735 ILCS 5/8-1206. Sworn Copies 237

§ 735 ILCS 5/8-1501. Comparison 237
§ 735 ILCS 5/8-1901. Admission of Liability — Effect 237
§ 735 ILCS 5/8-2601. Out-of-Court Statement 238
§ 740 ILCS 110/10. Disclosure in Civil, Criminal, and Other Proceedings 239
§ 810 ILCS 5/2-724. Admissibility of Market Quotations 248

Illinois Supreme Court Rules

Rule 212. Use of Depositions 249
Rule 213. Written Interrogatories to Parties . 249
Rule 216. Admission of Fact or of Genuineness of Documents 252
Rule 220. [Repealed/Reserved] 252
Rule 236. Admission of Business Records in Evidence 252
Rule 238. Impeachment of Witnesses; Hostile Witnesses 252
Rule 402. Pleas of Guilty or Stipulations Sufficient to Convict 253
Rule 433. Impeachment of Witnesses; Hostile Witnesses 253

Illinois Compiled Statutes

§ 225 ILCS 20/16. Privileged Communications and Exceptions

1. No licensed clinical social worker or licensed social worker shall disclose any information acquired from persons consulting the social worker in a professional capacity, except that which may be voluntarily disclosed under the following circumstances:

(a) In the course of formally reporting, conferring or consulting with administrative superiors, colleagues or consultants who share professional responsibility, in which instance all recipients of such information are similarly bound to regard the communication as privileged;

(b) With the written consent of the person who provided the information;

(c) In case of death or disability, with the written consent of a personal representative, other person authorized to sue, or the beneficiary of an insurance policy on the person's life, health or physical condition;

(d) When a communication reveals the intended commission of a crime or harmful act and such disclosure is judged necessary by the licensed clinical social worker or licensed social worker to protect any person from a clear, imminent risk of serious mental or physical harm or injury, or to forestall a serious threat to the public safety;

(e) When the person waives the privilege by bringing any public charges against the licensee; or

(f) When the information is acquired during the course of investigating a report or working on a case of elder abuse, neglect, or financial exploitation by a designated Elder Abuse Provider Agency and disclosure of the information is in accordance with the provisions of Section 8 of the Elder Abuse and Neglect Act [320 ILCS 20/8].

2. When the person is a minor under the laws of the State of Illinois and the information acquired by the licensed clinical social worker or licensed social worker indicates the minor was the victim or subject of a crime, the licensed clinical social worker or licensed social worker may be required to testify in any judicial proceedings in which the commission of that crime is the subject of inquiry and when, after in camera review of the information that the licensed clinical social worker or licensed social worker acquired, the court determines that the interests of the minor in having the information held privileged are outweighed by the requirements of justice, the need to protect the public safety or the need to protect the minor,

§ 225 ILCS 450/27.

except as provided under the Abused and Neglected Child Reporting Act [325 ILCS 5/1 et seq.].

3. Any person having access to records or any one who participates in providing social work services or who, in providing any human services, is supervised by a licensed clinical social worker or licensed social worker, is similarly bound to regard all information and communications as privileged in accord with this Section.

4. Nothing shall be construed to prohibit a licensed clinical social worker or licensed social worker from voluntarily testifying in court hearings concerning matters of adoption, child abuse, child neglect or other matters pertaining to children, except as provided under the Abused and Neglected Child Reporting Act [325 ILCS 5/1 et seq.].

5. The Mental Health and Developmental Disabilities Confidentiality Act, as now or hereafter amended [740 ILCS 110/1 et seq.], is incorporated herein as if all of its provisions were included in this Act.

§ 225 ILCS 450/27. Confidential Information

A public accountant shall not be required by any court to divulge information or evidence which has been obtained by him in his confidential capacity as a public accountant. This Section shall not apply

§ 305 ILCS 5 / 10-13.4.

to any investigation or hearing undertaken pursuant to this Act.

§ 305 ILCS 5/10-13.4. Proof of Records

The books, papers, records and memoranda of the Illinois Department or of the administrative enforcement unit, or parts thereof, may be proved in any hearing, investigation, or legal proceeding by a photostatic or other copy thereof under the certificate of the Director of the Illinois Department. Such certified copy shall, without further proof, be admitted into evidence in the hearing before the Illinois Department or in any other legal proceeding.

§ 410 ILCS 535/1. Definitions

As used in this Act, unless the context otherwise requires:

(1) "Vital records" means records of births, deaths, fetal deaths, marriages, dissolution of marriages, and data related thereto.

(2) "System of vital records" includes the registration, collection, preservation, amendment, and certification of vital records, and activities related thereto.

(3) "Filing" means the presentation of a certificate, report, or other record provided for in this Act, of a birth, death, fetal death, adoption, marriage,

§ 410 ILCS 535/1.

or dissolution of marriage, for registration by the Office of Vital Records.

(4) "Registration" means that acceptance by the Office of Vital Records and the incorporation in its official records of certificates, reports, or other records provided for in this Act, of births, deaths, fetal deaths, adoptions, marriages, or dissolution of marriages.

(5) "Live birth" means the complete expulsion or extraction from its mother of a product of human conception, irrespective of the duration of pregnancy, which after such separation breathes or shows any other evidence of life such as beating of the heart, pulsation of the umbilical cord, or definite movement of voluntary muscles, whether or not the umbilical cord has been cut or the placenta is attached.

(6) "Fetal death" means death prior to the complete expulsion or extraction from its mother of a product of human conception, irrespective of the duration of pregnancy; the death is indicated by the fact that after such separation the fetus does not breathe or show any other evidence of life such as beating of the heart, pulsation of the umbilical cord, or definite movement of voluntary muscles.

(7) "Dead body" means a lifeless human body or parts of such body or bones thereof from the state of which it may reasonably be concluded that death has occurred.

§ 725 ILCS 5/104-14.

(8) "Final disposition" means the burial, cremation, or other disposition of a dead human body or fetus or parts thereof.

(9) "Physician" means a person licensed to practice medicine in Illinois or any other State.

(10) "Institution" means any establishment, public or private, which provides in-patient medical, surgical, or diagnostic care or treatment, or nursing, custodial, or domiciliary care to 2 or more unrelated individuals, or to which persons are committed by law.

(11) "Department" means the Department of Public Health of the State of Illinois.

(12) "Director" means the Director of the Illinois Department of Public Health.

§ 725 ILCS 5/104-14. Use of Statements Made During Examination or Treatment

(a) Statements made by the defendant and information gathered in the course of any examination or treatment ordered under Section 104-13, 104-17 or 104-20 [725 ILCS 5/104-13, 725 ILCS 5/104-17 or 725 ILCS 5/104-20] shall not be admissible against the defendant unless he raises the defense of insanity or the defense of drugged or intoxicated condition, in which case they shall be admissible only on the issue of whether he was insane, drugged, or intoxicated. The refusal of the defendant to cooperate in such examinations shall

§ 725 ILCS 5/104-14.

not preclude the raising of the aforesaid defenses but shall preclude the defendant from offering expert evidence or testimony tending to support such defenses if the expert evidence or testimony is based upon the expert's examination of the defendant.

(b) Except as provided in paragraph (a) of this Section, no statement made by the defendant in the course of any examination or treatment ordered under Section 104-13, 104-17 or 104-20 [725 ILCS 5/104-13, 725 ILCS 5/104-17 or 725 ILCS 5/104-20] which relates to the crime charged or to other criminal acts shall be disclosed by persons conducting the examination or the treatment, except to members of the examining or treating team, without the informed written consent of the defendant, who is competent at the time of giving such consent.

(c) The court shall advise the defendant of the limitations on the use of any statements made or information gathered in the course of the fitness examination or subsequent treatment as provided in this Section. It shall also advise him that he may refuse to cooperate with the person conducting the examination, but that his refusal may be admissible into evidence on the issue of his mental or physical condition.

§ 725 ILCS 5/115-5. Business Records as Evidence

(a) Any writing or record, whether in the form of an entry in a book or otherwise, made as a memorandum or record of any act, transaction, occurrence, or event, shall be admissible as evidence of such act, transaction, occurrence, or event, if made in regular course of any business, and if it was the regular course of such business to make such memorandum or record at the time of such act, transaction, occurrence, or event or within a reasonable time thereafter.

All other circumstances of the making of such writing or record, including lack of personal knowledge by the entrant or maker, may be shown to affect its weight, but such circumstances shall not affect its admissibility.

The term "business," as used in this Section, includes business, profession, occupation, and calling of every kind.

(b) If any business, institution, member of a profession or calling, or any department or agency of government, in the regular course of business or activity has kept or recorded any memorandum, writing, entry, print, representation or combination thereof, of any act, transaction, occurrence, or event, and in the regular course of business has caused any or all of the same to be recorded, copied, or reproduced by any photographic, photostatic,

§ 725 ILCS 5/115-5.

microfilm, micro-card, miniature photographic, optical imaging, or other process which accurately reproduces or forms a medium for so reproducing the original, the original may be destroyed in the regular course of business unless its preservation is required by law. Such reproduction, when satisfactorily identified, is as admissible in evidence as the original itself in any proceeding whether the original is in existence or not and an enlargement or facsimile of such reproduction is likewise admissible in evidence if the original reproduction is in existence and available for inspection under direction of court. The introduction of a reproduced record, enlargement, or facsimile does not preclude admission of the original. This Section shall not be construed to exclude from evidence any document or copy thereof which is otherwise admissible under the rules of evidence.

(c) No writing or record made in the regular course of any business shall become admissible as evidence by the application of this Section if:

(1) Such writing or record has been made by anyone in the regular course of any form of hospital or medical business; or

(2) Such writing or record has been made by anyone during an investigation of an alleged offense or during any investigation relating to pending or anticipated litigation of any kind.

§ 725 ILCS 5 / 115-5.1.

§ 725 ILCS 5/115-5.1. Coroner's Records as Evidence

In any civil or criminal action the records of the coroner's medical or laboratory examiner summarizing and detailing the performance of his or her official duties in performing medical examinations upon deceased persons or autopsies, or both, and kept in the ordinary course of business of the coroner's office, duly certified by the county coroner or chief supervisory coroner's pathologist or medical examiner, shall be received as competent evidence in any court of this State, to the extent permitted by this Section. These reports, specifically including but not limited to the pathologist's protocol, autopsy reports and toxicological reports, shall be public documents and thereby may be admissible as prima facie evidence of the facts, findings, opinions, diagnoses and conditions stated therein.

A duly certified coroner's protocol or autopsy report, or both, complying with the requirements of this Section may be duly admitted into evidence as an exception to the hearsay rule as prima facie proof of the cause of death of the person to whom it relates. The records referred to in this Section shall be limited to the records of the results of post-mortem examinations of the findings of autopsy and toxicological laboratory examinations.

§ 725 ILCS 5 / 115-7.

Persons who prepare reports or records offered in evidence hereunder may be subpoenaed as witnesses in civil or criminal cases upon the request of either party to the cause. However, if such person is dead, the county coroner or a duly authorized official of the coroner's office may testify to the fact that the examining pathologist, toxicologist or other medical or laboratory examiner is deceased and that the offered report or record was prepared by such deceased person. The witness must further attest that the medical report or record was prepared in the ordinary and usual course of the deceased person's duty or employment in conformity with the provisions of this Section.

§ 725 ILCS 5/115-7. Prior Sexual Activity or Reputation of Victim of Sexual Offense (Effective January 1, 1998)

a. In prosecutions for predatory criminal sexual assault of a child, aggravated criminal sexual assault, criminal sexual assault, aggravated criminal sexual abuse, criminal sexual abuse, or criminal transmission of HIV; and in prosecutions for battery and aggravated battery, when the commission of the offense involves sexual penetration or sexual conduct as defined in Section 12-12 of the Criminal Code of 1961 [720 ILCS 5/12-12]; and with the trial or retrial of the offenses formerly known as rape, deviate sexual assault, indecent

§ 725 ILCS 5 / 115-7.

liberties with a child, and aggravated indecent liberties with a child, the prior sexual activity or the reputation of the alleged victim or corroborating witness under Section 115-7.3 of this Code [725 ILCS 5/115-7.3] is inadmissible except (1) as evidence concerning the past sexual conduct of the alleged victim or corroborating witness under Section 115-7.3 of this Code [725 ILCS 5/115-7.3] with the accused when this evidence is offered by the accused upon the issue of whether the alleged victim or corroborating witness under Section 115-7.3 of this Code [725 ILCS 5/115-7.3] consented to the sexual conduct with respect to which the offense is alleged; or (2) when constitutionally required to be admitted.

b. No evidence admissible under this Section shall be introduced unless ruled admissible by the trial judge after an offer of proof has been made at a hearing to be held in camera in order to determine whether the defense has evidence to impeach the witness in the event that prior sexual activity with the defendant is denied. Such offer of proof shall include reasonably specific information as to the date, time and place of the past sexual conduct between the alleged victim or corroborating witness under Section 115-7.3 of this Code [725 ILCS 5/115-7.3] and the defendant. Unless the court finds that reasonably specific information as to date, time or place, or some combination thereof,

§ 725 ILCS 5/115-7.3.

has been offered as to prior sexual activity with the defendant, counsel for the defendant shall be ordered to refrain from inquiring into prior sexual activity between the alleged victim or corroborating witness under Section 115-7.3 of this Code [725 ILCS 5/115-7.3] and the defendant. The court shall not admit evidence under this Section unless it determines at the hearing that the evidence is relevant and the probative value of the evidence outweighs the danger of unfair prejudice. The evidence shall be admissible at trial to the extent an order made by the court specifies the evidence that may be admitted and areas with respect to which the alleged victim or corroborating witness under Section 115-7.3 of this Code [725 ILCS 5/115-7.3] may be examined or cross examined.

§ 725 ILCS 5/115-7.3. Evidence in Certain Cases

(a) This Section applies to criminal cases in which:

(1) The defendant is accused of predatory criminal sexual assault of a child, aggravated criminal sexual assault, criminal sexual assault, aggravated criminal sexual abuse, criminal sexual abuse, or criminal transmission of HIV;

(2) The defendant is accused of battery or aggravated battery when the commission of the offense involves sexual penetration or sexual

§ 725 ILCS 5 / 115-7.3.

conduct as defined in Section 12-12 of the Criminal Code of 1961; or

(3) The defendant is tried or retried for any of the offenses formerly known as rape, deviate sexual assault, indecent liberties with a child, or aggravated indecent liberties with a child.

(b) If the defendant is accused of an offense set forth in paragraph (1) or (2) of subsection (a) or the defendant is tried or retried for any of the offenses set forth in paragraph (3) of subsection (a), evidence of the defendant's commission of another offense or offenses set forth in paragraph (1), (2), or (3) of subsection (a), or evidence to rebut that proof or an inference from that proof, may be admissible (if that evidence is otherwise admissible under the rules of evidence) and may be considered for its bearing on any matter to which it is relevant.

(c) In weighing the probative value of the evidence against undue prejudice to the defendant, the court may consider:

(1) the proximity in time to the charged or predicate offense;

(2) the degree of factual similarity to the charged or predicate offense; or

(3) other relevant facts and circumstances.

(d) In a criminal case in which the prosecution intends to offer evidence under this Section, it

§ 725 ILCS 5 / 115-10.

must disclose the evidence, including statements of witnesses or a summary of the substance of any testimony, at a reasonable time in advance of trial, or during trial if the court excuses pretrial notice on good cause shown.

(e) In a criminal case in which evidence is offered under this Section, proof may be made by specific instances of conduct, testimony as to reputation, or testimony in the form of an expert opinion, except that the prosecution may offer reputation testimony only after the opposing party has offered that testimony.

§ 725 ILCS 5/115-10. Certain Hearsay Exceptions

(a) In a prosecution for a physical or sexual act perpetrated upon or against a child under the age of 13, or a person who was an institutionalized severely or profoundly mentally retarded person as defined in Section 2-10.1 of the Criminal Code of 1961 [720 ILCS 5/2-10.1] at the time the act was committed, including but not limited to prosecutions for violations of Sections 12-13 through 12-16 of the Criminal Code of 1961 [720 ILCS 5/12-13 through 720 ILCS 5/12-16 and prosecutions for violations of Sections 10-1, 10-2, 10-3, 10-3.1, 10-4, 10-5, 10-6, 10-7, 11-6, 11-9, 11-11, 11-15.1, 11-17.1, 11-18.1, 11-19.1, 11-19.2, 11-20.1, 11-21, 12-1, 12-2, 12-3, 12-3.2, 12-4, 12-4.1, 12-4.2, 12-4.3, 12-4.7,

§ 725 ILCS 5 / 115-10.

12-5, 12-6, 12-6.1, 12-7.1, 12-7.3, 12-7.4, 12-10, 12-11, 12-21.5, 12-21.6 and 12-32 of the Criminal Code of 1961 [720 ILCS 5/10-1, 720 ILCS 5/10-2, 720 ILCS 5/10-3, 720 ILCS 5/10-3.1, 720 ILCS 5/10-4, 720 ILCS 5/10-5, 720 ILCS 5/10-6, 720 ILCS 5/10-7, 720 ILCS 5/11-6, 720 ILCS 5/11-9, 720 ILCS 5/11-11, 720 ILCS 5/11-15.1, 720 ILCS 5/11-17.1, 720 ILCS 5/11-18.1, 720 ILCS 5/11-19.1, 720 ILCS 5/11-19.2, 720 ILCS 5/11-20.1, 720 ILCS 5/11-21, 720 ILCS 5/12-1, 720 ILCS 5/12-2, 720 ILCS 5/12-3, 720 ILCS 5/12-3.2, 720 ILCS 5/12-4, 720 ILCS 5/12-4.1, 720 ILCS 5/12-4.2, 720 ILCS 5/12-4.3, 720 ILCS 5/12-4.7, 720 ILCS 5/12-5, 720 ILCS 5/12-6, 720 ILCS 5/12-6.1, 720 ILCS 5/12-7.1, 720 ILCS 5/12-7.3, 720 ILCS 5/12-7.4, 720 ILCS 5/12-10, 720 ILCS 5/12-11, 720 ILCS 5/12-21.5, 720 ILCS 5/12-21.6 and 720 ILCS 5/12-32], the following evidence shall be admitted as an exception to the hearsay rule:

(1) testimony by such child or institutionalized severely or profoundly mentally retarded person, of an out of court statement made by such child or institutionalized severely or profoundly mentally retarded person, that he or she complained of such act to another; and

(2) testimony of an out of court statement made by such child or institutionalized severely or profoundly mentally retarded person, describing any complaint of such act or matter or

§ 725 ILCS 5/115-10.

detail pertaining to any act which is an element of an offense which is the subject of a prosecution for a sexual or physical act perpetrated upon or against a child or institutionalized severely or profoundly mentally retarded person.

(b) Such testimony shall only be admitted if:

(1) The court finds in a hearing conducted outside the presence of the jury that the time, content, and circumstances of the statement provide sufficient safeguards of reliability; and

(2) The child or institutionalized severely or profoundly mentally retarded person either:

(A) testifies at the proceeding; or

(B) is unavailable as a witness and there is corroborative evidence of the act which is the subject of the statement.

(c) If a statement is admitted pursuant to this Section, the court shall instruct the jury that it is for the jury to determine the weight and credibility to be given the statement and that, in making the determination, it shall consider the age and maturity of the child, or the intellectual capabilities of the institutionalized severely or profoundly mentally retarded person, the nature of the statement, the circumstances under which the statement was made, and any other relevant factor.

(d) The proponent of the statement shall give the adverse party reasonable notice of his inten-

§ 725 ILCS 5/115-10.1.

tion to offer the statement and the particulars of the statement.

(e) Statements described in paragraphs (1) and (2) of subsection (a) shall not be excluded on the basis that they were obtained as a result of interviews conducted pursuant to a protocol adopted by a Child Advocacy Advisory Board as set forth in subsections (c), (d), and (e) of Section 3 of the Children's Advocacy Center Act [55 ILCS 80/3] or that an interviewer or witness to the interview was or is an employee, agent, or investigator of a State's Attorney's office.

§ 725 ILCS 5/115-10.1. Admissibility of Prior Inconsistent Statements

In all criminal cases, evidence of a statement made by a witness is not made inadmissible by the hearsay rule if

(a) the statement is inconsistent with his testimony at the hearing or trial, and

(b) the witness is subject to cross-examination concerning the statement, and

(c) the statement —

(1) was made under oath at a trial, hearing, or other proceeding, or

(2) narrates, describes, or explains an event or condition of which the witness had personal knowledge, and

    (A) the statement is proved to have been written or signed by the witness, or

    (B) the witness acknowledged under oath the making of the statement either in his testimony at the hearing or trial in which the admission into evidence of the prior statement is being sought, or at a trial, hearing, or other proceeding, or

    (C) the statement is proved to have been accurately recorded by a tape recorder, videotape recording, or any other similar electronic means of sound recording.

Nothing in this Section shall render a prior inconsistent statement inadmissible for purposes of impeachment because such statement was not recorded or otherwise fails to meet the criteria set forth herein.

§ 725 ILCS 5/115-10.2. Admissibility of Prior Statements When Witness Refused to Testify Despite a Court Order to Testify

(a) A statement not specifically covered by any other hearsay exception but having equivalent circumstantial guarantees of trustworthiness, is not excluded by the hearsay rule if the declarant is

§ 725 ILCS 5 / 115-10.2.

unavailable as defined in subsection (c) and if the court determines that:

(1) the statement is offered as evidence of a material fact; and

(2) the statement is more probative on the point for which it is offered than any other evidence which the proponent can procure through reasonable efforts; and

(3) the general purposes of this Section and the interests of justice will best be served by admission of the statement into evidence.

(b) A statement may not be admitted under this exception unless the proponent of it makes known to the adverse party sufficiently in advance of the trial or hearing to provide the adverse party with a fair opportunity to prepare to meet it, the proponent's intention to offer the statement, and the particulars of the statement, including the name and address of the declarant.

(c) Unavailability as a witness is limited to the situation in which the declarant persists in refusing to testify concerning the subject matter of the declarant's statement despite an order of the court to do so.

(d) A declarant is not unavailable as a witness if exemption, refusal, claim or lack of memory, inability or absence is due to the procurement or wrongdoing of the proponent of a statement for

§ 725 ILCS 5/115-14.

purpose of preventing the witness from attending or testifying.

(e) Nothing in this Section shall render a prior statement inadmissible for purposes of impeachment because the statement was not recorded or otherwise fails to meet the criteria set forth in this Section.

§ 725 ILCS 5/115-13. Medical Records as Evidence in Trial for Sexual Offense

In a prosecution for violation of Section 12-13, 12-14, 12-14.1, 12-15 or 12-16 of the "Criminal Code of 1961" [720 ILCS 5/12-13, 720 ILCS 5/12-14, 720 ILCS 5/12-14.1, 720 ILCS 5/12-15 or 720 ILCS 5/12-16], statements made by the victim to medical personnel for purposes of medical diagnosis or treatment including descriptions of the cause of symptom, pain or sensations, or the inception or general character of the cause or external source thereof insofar as reasonably pertinent to diagnosis or treatment shall be admitted as an exception to the hearsay rule.

§ 725 ILCS 5/115-14. Witness Competency

(a) Every person, irrespective of age, is qualified to be a witness and no person is disqualified to testify to any matter, except as provided in subsection (b).

§ 725 ILCS 5/115-15.

(b) A person is disqualified to be a witness if he or she is:

(1) Incapable of expressing himself or herself concerning the matter so as to be understood, either directly or through interpretation by one who can understand him or her; or

(2) Incapable of understanding the duty of a witness to tell the truth.

(c) A party may move the court prior to a witness' testimony being received in evidence, requesting that the court make a determination if a witness is competent to testify. The hearing shall be conducted outside the presence of the jury and the burden of proof shall be on the moving party.

§ 725 ILCS 5/115-15. Laboratory Reports (Effective January 1, 1998)

(a) In any criminal prosecution for a violation of either the Cannabis Control Act [720 ILCS 550/1 et seq.] or the Illinois Controlled Substances Act [720 ILCS 570/100 et seq.], a laboratory report from the Department of State Police, Division of Forensic Services, that is signed and sworn to by the person performing an analysis and that states (1) that the substance that is the basis of the alleged violation has been weighed and analyzed, and (2) the person's findings as to the contents, weight and identity of the substance, and (3) that it contains any amount of a controlled substance

§ 725 ILCS 5/115-15.

or cannabis is prima facie evidence of the contents, identity and weight of the substance. Attached to the report shall be a copy of a notarized statement by the signer of the report giving the name of the signer and stating (i) that he or she is an employee of the Department of State Police, Division of Forensic Services, (ii) the name and location of the laboratory where the analysis was performed, (iii) that performing the analysis is a part of his or her regular duties, and (iv) that the signer is qualified by education, training and experience to perform the analysis. The signer shall also allege that scientifically accepted tests were performed with due caution and that the evidence was handled in accordance with established and accepted procedures while in the custody of the laboratory.

(b) The State's Attorney shall serve a copy of the report on the attorney of record for the accused, or on the accused if he or she has no attorney, before any proceeding in which the report is to be used against the accused other than at a preliminary hearing or grand jury hearing when the report may be used without having been previously served upon the accused.

(c) The report shall not be prima facie evidence of the contents, identity, and weight of the substance if the accused or his or her attorney demands the testimony of the person signing the report by serving the demand upon the State's

§ 735 ILCS 5/2-1002.

Attorney within 7 days from the accused or his or her attorney's receipt of the report.

§ 735 ILCS 5/2-1002. [Repealed]

Repealed by P.A. 87-949, § 2, effective January 1, 1993.

§ 735 ILCS 5/2-1102. Examination of Adverse Party or Agent

Upon the trial of any case any party thereto or any person for whose immediate benefit the action is prosecuted or defended, or the officers, directors, managing agents or foreman of any party to the action, may be called and examined as if under cross-examination at the instance of any adverse party. The party calling for the examination is not concluded thereby but may rebut the testimony thus given by countertestimony and may impeach the witness by proof of prior inconsistent statements.

§ 735 ILCS 5/8-101. Interested Witness

No person shall be disqualified as a witness in any action or proceeding, except as hereinafter stated, by reason of his or her interest in the event thereof, as a party or otherwise, or by reason of his or her conviction of any crime; but such interest or conviction may be shown for the purpose of affecting the credibility of such witness; and the fact of such conviction may be proven like any fact not of record, either by the witness himself or herself (who shall be compelled to testify thereto) or by any other witness cognizant of such conviction, as impeaching testimony, or by any other competent evidence.

§ 735 ILCS 5/8-201. Dead Man's Act

In the trial of any action in which any party sues or defends as the representative of a deceased person or person under a legal disability, no adverse party or person directly interested in the action shall be allowed to testify on his or her own behalf to any conversation with the deceased or person under legal disability or to any event which took place in the presence of the deceased or person under legal disability, except in the following instances:

(a) If any person testifies on behalf of the representative to any conversation with the deceased or person under legal disability or to any event which took place in the presence of the deceased or person under legal disability, any adverse party or interested person, if otherwise competent, may testify concerning the same conversation or event.

(b) If the deposition of the deceased or person under legal disability is admitted in evidence on behalf of the representative, any adverse party or interested person, if otherwise competent, may

§ 735 ILCS 5/8-201.

testify concerning the same matters admitted in evidence.

(c) Any testimony competent under Section 8-401 of this Act [735 ILCS 5/8-401], is not barred by this Section.

(d) No person shall be barred from testifying as to any fact relating to the heirship of a decedent.

As used in this Section:

(a) "Person under legal disability" means any person who is adjudged by the court in the pending civil action to be unable to testify by reason of mental illness, mental retardation or deterioration of mentality.

(b) "Representative" means an executor, administrator, heir or legatee of a deceased person and any guardian or trustee of any such heir or legatee, or a guardian or guardian ad litem for a person under legal disability.

(c) "Person directly interested in the action" or "interested person" does not include a person who is interested solely as executor, trustee or in any other fiduciary capacity, whether or not he or she receives or expects to receive compensation for acting in that capacity.

(d) This Section applies to proceedings filed on or after October 1, 1973.

§ 735 ILCS 5/8-401. Account Books and Records

Where in any action or proceeding, the claim or defense is founded on a book account or any other record or document, any party or interested person may testify to his or her account book, or any other record or document and the items therein contained; that the same is a book, record, or document of original entries, and that the entries therein were made by himself or herself, and are true and just; or that the same were made by a deceased person, or by a disinterested person, a non-resident person of the state at the time of the trial, and where made by such deceased or non-resident person in the usual course of trade, and of his or her duty or employment to the party so testifying; and thereupon the account book and entries or any other record or document shall be admitted as evidence in the cause. Where such book of original entries or any other record or document has been photographed, microphotographed, microfilmed, optical imaged, or otherwise reproduced either in the usual course of business, or pursuant to any statute of this State authorizing the reproduction of public records, papers or documents, and the reproduction, in either case, complies with the minimum standards of quality for permanent records approved by the State Records Commission, then such reproduction

§ 735 ILCS 5/8-801.

shall be deemed to be an original record, book or document for all purposes, including introduction in evidence in all courts or administrative agencies.

§ 735 ILCS 5/8-801. Husband and Wife

In all actions, husband and wife may testify for or against each other, provided that neither may testify as to any communication or admission made by either of them to the other or as to any conversation between them during marriage, except in actions between such husband and wife, and in actions where the custody, support, health or welfare of their children or children in either spouse's care, custody or control is directly in issue, and as to matters in which either has acted as agent for the other.

§ 735 ILCS 5/8-802. Healthcare Practitioner and Patient

No physician, surgeon, psychologist, nurse, mental health worker, therapist, or other healing art practitioner (referred to in this Section as "healthcare practitioner") shall be permitted to disclose any information he or she may have acquired in attending any patient in a professional character, necessary to enable him or her professionally to serve the patient, except only (1) in trials for homicide when the disclosure relates

§ 735 ILCS 5/8-802.

directly to the fact or immediate circumstances of the homicide, (2) in actions, civil or criminal, against the healthcare practitioner for malpractice (in which instance the patient shall be deemed to have waived all privileges relating to physical or mental condition), (3) with the expressed consent of the patient, or in case of his or her death or disability, of his or her personal representative or other person authorized to sue for personal injury or of the beneficiary of an insurance policy on his or her life, health, or physical condition, (4) in all actions brought by the patient, his or her personal representative, a beneficiary under a policy of insurance, or the executor or administrator of his or her estate wherein the patient's physical or mental condition is an issue (in which instance the patient shall be deemed to have waived all privileges relating to physical or mental condition), (4.1) in all actions brought against the patient, his or her personal representative, a beneficiary under a policy of insurance, or the executor or administrator of his or her estate wherein the patient's physical or mental condition is an issue, (5) upon an issue as the validity of a document as a will of the patient, (6) in any criminal action where the charge is either first degree murder by abortion, attempted abortion or abortion, (7) in actions, civil or criminal arising from the filing of a report in compliance with the Abused and Neglected Child Reporting Act [325 ILCS 5/1 et seq.], (8) to any

§ 735 ILCS 5 / 8-802.

department, agency, institution or facility which has custody of the patient pursuant to State statute or any court order of commitment, (9) in prosecutions where written results of blood alcohol tests are admissible pursuant to Section 11-501.4 of the Illinois Vehicle Code [625 ILCS 5/11-501.4] or (10) in prosecutions where written results of blood alcohol tests are admissible under Section 5-11a of the Boat Registration and Safety Act [625 ILCS 45/5-11a].

In all instances where a patient or the patient's representative seeks damages for personal injury, death, pain and suffering, or mental or emotional injury and where a written request pursuant to Section 2-1003 [735 ILCS 5/2-1003] has been made, then (1) the healthcare practitioner is authorized to provide information regarding the patient to attorneys for any of the parties in pending civil, criminal, or administrative proceedings in written or verbal form as described in Section 2-1003 [735 ILCS 5/2-1003] and (2) any attorney for any party in any civil, criminal, or administrative action brought by or against a patient, his or her personal representative, a beneficiary under a policy of insurance, or the executor or administrator of his or her estate wherein the patient's physical or mental condition is an issue may obtain in written or verbal form as described in Section 2-1003 [735 ILCS 5/2-1003] any information that

§ 735 ILCS 5/8-802.

any healthcare practitioner has acquired in attending to the patient in a professional character. Nothing in this Section shall preclude or limit any formal discovery.

A health care practitioner, as defined in Section 2-1003 [735 ILCS 5/2-1003], shall have the right to (1) communicate at any time and in any fashion with his or her own counsel and professional liability insurer concerning any care or treatment he or she provided, or assisted in providing, to any patient and (2) communicate at any time and in any fashion with his or her present or former employer, principal, partner, professional corporation, professional liability insurer, or counsel for the same, concerning care or treatment he or she provided, or assisted in providing, to any patient during the pendency and within the scope of his or her employment or affiliation with the employer, principal, partner, or professional corporation.

In the event of a conflict between the application of this Section and the Mental Health and Developmental Disabilities Confidentiality Act [740 ILCS 110/1 et seq.] to a specific situation, the provisions of the Mental Health and Developmental Disabilities Confidentiality Act [740 ILCS 110/1 et seq.] shall control.

This amendatory Act of 1995 applies to causes of action filed on or after its effective date.

§ 735 ILCS 5/8-802.1. Confidentiality of Statements Made to Rape Crisis Personnel

(a) Purpose. This Section is intended to protect victims of rape from public disclosure of statements they make in confidence to counselors of organizations established to help them. On or after July 1, 1984, "rape" means an act of forced sexual penetration or sexual conduct, as defined in Section 12-12 of the Criminal Code of 1961, as amended [720 ILCS 5/12-12], including acts prohibited under Sections 12-13 through 12-16 of the Criminal Code of 1961, as amended [720 ILCS 5/12-13 through 720 ILCS 5/12-16]. Because of the fear and stigma that often results from those crimes, many victims hesitate to seek help even where it is available at no cost to them. As a result they not only fail to receive needed medical care and emergency counseling, but may lack the psychological support necessary to report the crime and aid police in preventing future crimes.

(b) Definitions. As used in this Act:

(1) "Rape crisis organization" means any organization or association the major purpose of which is providing information, counseling, and psychological support to victims of any or all of the crimes of aggravated criminal sexual assault, predatory criminal sexual assault of a child, criminal sexual assault, sexual relations

§ 735 ILCS 5/8-802.1.

between siblings, criminal sexual abuse and aggravated criminal sexual abuse.

(2) "Rape crisis counselor" means a person who is a psychologist, social worker, employee, or volunteer in any organization or association defined as a rape crisis organization under this Section, who has undergone 40 hours of training and is under the control of a direct services supervisor of a rape crisis organization.

(3) "Victim" means a person who is the subject of, or who seeks information, counseling, or advocacy services as a result of an aggravated criminal sexual assault, predatory criminal sexual assault of a child, criminal sexual assault, sexual relations within families, criminal sexual abuse, aggravated criminal sexual abuse, sexual exploitation of a child, indecent solicitation of a child, public indecency, exploitation of a child, or an attempt to commit any of these offenses.

(4) "Confidential communication" means any communication between a victim and a rape crisis counselor in the course of providing information, counseling, and advocacy. The term includes all records kept by the counselor or by the organization in the course of providing services to an alleged victim concerning the alleged victim and the services provided.

§ 735 ILCS 5/8-802.1.

(c) Waiver of privilege.

(1) The confidential nature of the communication is not waived by: the presence of a third person who further expresses the interests of the victim at the time of the communication; group counseling; or disclosure to a third person with the consent of the victim when reasonably necessary to accomplish the purpose for which the counselor is consulted.

(2) The confidential nature of counseling records is not waived when: the victim inspects the records; or in the case of a minor child less than 12 years of age, a parent or guardian whose interests are not adverse to the minor inspects the records; or in the case of a minor victim 12 years or older, a parent or guardian whose interests are not adverse to the minor inspects the records with the victim's consent.

(3) When a victim is deceased or has been adjudged incompetent by a court of competent jurisdiction, the victim's guardian or the executor or administrator of the victim's estate may waive the privilege established by this Section, unless the guardian, executor, or administrator has an interest adverse to the victim.

(4) A minor victim 12 years of age or older may knowingly waive the privilege established in this Section. When a minor is, in the opinion of the Court, incapable of knowingly waiving the

§ 735 ILCS 5/8-802.1.

privilege, the parent or guardian of the minor may waive the privilege on behalf of the minor, unless the parent or guardian has been charged with a violent crime against the victim or otherwise has any interest adverse to that of the minor with respect to the waiver of the privilege.

(d) Confidentiality. Except as provided in this Act, no rape crisis counselor shall disclose any confidential communication or be examined as a witness in any civil or criminal proceeding as to any confidential communication without the written consent of the victim or a representative of the victim as provided in subparagraph (c).

(e) A rape crisis counselor may disclose a confidential communication without the consent of the victim if failure to disclose is likely to result in a clear, imminent risk of serious physical injury or death of the victim or another person. Any rape crisis counselor or rape crisis organization participating in good faith in the disclosing of records and communications under this Act shall have immunity from any liability, civil, criminal, or otherwise that might result from the action. In any proceeding, civil or criminal, arising out of a disclosure under this Section, the good faith of any rape crisis counselor or rape crisis organization who disclosed the confidential communication shall be presumed.

§ 735 ILCS 5/8-802.2.

(f) Any rape crisis counselor who knowingly discloses any confidential communication in violation of this Act commits a Class C misdemeanor.

§ 735 ILCS 5/8-802.2. Confidentiality of Statements Made to Personnel Counseling Victims of Violent Crimes

(a) Purpose. This Section is intended to protect victims of violent crimes from public disclosure of statements they make in confidence to counselors of organizations established to help them. Because of the fear and trauma that often results from violent crimes, many victims hesitate to seek help even where it is available and may therefore lack the psychological support necessary to report the crime and aid police in preventing future crimes.

(b) Definitions. As used in this Act, "violent crimes" include, but are not limited to, any felony in which force or threat of force was used against the victim or any misdemeanor which results in death or great bodily harm to the victim.

(c) Confidentiality. Where any victim of a violent crime makes a statement relating to the crime or its circumstances during the course of therapy or consultation to any counselor, employee or volunteer of a victim aid organization, the statement or contents thereof shall not be disclosed by the organization or any of its personnel unless the

§ 735 ILCS 5/8-803.

maker of the statement consents in writing or unless otherwise directed pursuant to this Section.

If in any judicial proceeding, a party alleges that such statements are necessary to the determination of any issue before the court and written consent to disclosure has not been given, the party may ask the court to consider the relevance and admissibility of the statements. In such a case, the court shall hold a hearing in camera on the relevance of the statements. If the court finds them relevant and admissible to the issue, the court shall order the statements to be disclosed.

§ 735 ILCS 5/8-803. Clergy

A clergyman or practitioner of any religious denomination accredited by the religious body to which he or she belongs, shall not be compelled to disclose in any court, or to any administrative board or agency, or to any public officer, a confession or admission made to him or her in his or her professional character or as a spiritual advisor in the course of the discipline enjoined by the rules or practices of such religious body or of the religion which he or she professes, nor be compelled to divulge any information which has been obtained by him or her in such professional character or as such spiritual advisor.

§ 735 ILCS 5/8-901.

§ 735 ILCS 5/8-901. Source of Information

No court may compel any person to disclose the source of any information obtained by a reporter except as provided in Part 9 of Article VIII of this Act [735 ILCS 5/8-901 et seq.].

§ 735 ILCS 5/8-902. Definitions

(a) "reporter" means any person regularly engaged in the business of collecting, writing or editing news for publication through a news medium on a full-time or part-time basis; and includes any person who was a reporter at the time the information sought was procured or obtained.

(b) "news medium" means any newspaper or other periodical issued at regular intervals and having a general circulation; a news service; a radio station; a television station; a community antenna television service; and any person or corporation engaged in the making of news reels or other motion picture news for public showing.

(c) "source" means the person or means from or through which the news or information was obtained.

§ 735 ILCS 5/8-903. Application to Court

(a) In any case, except a libel or slander case, where a person claims the privilege conferred by Part 9 of Article VIII of this Act [735 ILCS 5/8-901 et seq.] the person or party, body or officer seeking

§ 735 ILCS 5/8-904.

the information so privileged may apply in writing to the circuit court serving the county where the hearing, action or proceeding in which the information is sought for an order divesting the person named therein of such privilege and ordering him or her to disclose his or her source of the information.

(b) In libel or slander cases where a person claims the privilege conferred by Part 9 of Article VIII of this Act [735 ILCS 5/8-901 et seq.], the plaintiff may apply in writing to the court for an order divesting the person named therein of such privilege and ordering him or her to disclose his or her source of information.

§ 735 ILCS 5/8-904. Contents of Application

The application provided in Section 8-903 of this Act [735 ILCS 5/8-903] shall allege: the name of the reporter and of the news medium with which he or she was connected at the time the information sought was obtained; the specific information sought and its relevancy to the proceedings; and, either, a specific public interest which would be adversely affected if the factual information sought were not disclosed, or, in libel or slander cases, the necessity of disclosure of the information sought to the proof of plaintiff's case. Additionally, in libel or slander cases, the plaintiff must include in the application provided in Section 8-903 [735

§ 735 ILCS 5/8-905.

ILCS 5/8-903] a prima facie showing of falsity of the alleged defamation and actual harm or injury due to the alleged defamation.

§ 735 ILCS 5/8-905. Civil Proceeding

All proceedings in connection with obtaining an adjudication upon the application not otherwise provided in Part 9 of Article VIII of this Act [735 ILCS 58-901 et seq.] shall be as in other civil cases.

§ 735 ILCS 5/8-906. Consideration by Court

In granting or denying divestiture of the privilege provided in Part 9 of Article VIII of this Act [735 ILCS 5/8-901 et seq.] the court shall have due regard to the nature of the proceedings, the merits of the claim or defense, the adequacy of the remedy otherwise available, if any, the relevancy of the source, and the possibility of establishing by other means that which it is alleged the source requested will tend to prove.

§ 735 ILCS 5/8-907. Court's Findings

An order granting divestiture of the privilege provided in Part 9 of Article VIII of this Act [735 ILCS 5/8-901 et seq.] shall be granted only if the court, after hearing the parties, finds:

(1) that the information sought does not concern matters, or details in any proceeding, required to

be kept secret under the laws of this State or of the Federal government; and

(2) that all other available sources of information have been exhausted and, either, disclosure of the information sought is essential to the protection of the public interest involved or, in libel or slander cases, the plaintiff's need for disclosure of the information sought outweighs the public interest in protecting the confidentiality of sources of information used by a reporter as part of the news gathering process under the particular facts and circumstances of each particular case.

If the court enters an order divesting the person of the privilege granted in Part 9 of Article VIII of this Act [735 ILCS 5/8-901 et seq.] it shall also order the person to disclose the information it has determined should be disclosed, subject to any protective conditions as the court may deem necessary or appropriate.

§ 735 ILCS 5/8-908. Privilege Continues During Pendency of Appeal

In case of an appeal the privilege conferred by Part 9 of Article VIII of this Act [735 ILCS 5/8-901 et seq.] remains in full force and effect during the pendency of such appeal.

§ 735 ILCS 5/8-909. Contempt

A person refusing to testify or otherwise comply with the order to disclose the source of the information as specified in such order, after such order becomes final, may be adjudged in contempt of court and punished accordingly.

§ 735 ILCS 5/8-1202. Court Records

The papers, entries and records of courts may be proved by a copy thereof certified under the signature of the clerk having the custody thereof, and the seal of the court, or by the judge of the court if there is no clerk.

§ 735 ILCS 5/8-1203. Municipal Records

The papers, entries, records and ordinances, or parts thereof, of any city, village, town or county, may be proved by a copy thereof, certified under the signature of the clerk or the keeper thereof, and the corporate seal, if there is any; if not, under his or her signature and private seal.

§ 735 ILCS 5/8-1204. Corporate Records

The papers, entries and records of any corporation or incorporated association may be proved by a copy thereof, certified under the signature of the secretary, clerk, cashier or other keeper of the same. If the corporation or

§ 735 ILCS 5/8-1901.

incorporated association has a seal, the same shall be affixed to such certificate.

§ 735 ILCS 5/8-1205. Form of Certificate

The certificate of any such clerk of a court, city, village, town, county, or secretary, clerk, cashier, or other keeper of any such papers, entries, records or ordinances, shall contain a statement that such person is the keeper of the same, and if there is no seal, shall so state.

§ 735 ILCS 5/8-1206. Sworn Copies

Any such papers, entries, records and ordinances may be proved by copies examined and sworn to by credible witnesses.

§ 735 ILCS 5/8-1501. Comparison

In all courts of this State it shall be lawful to prove handwriting by comparison made by the witness or jury with writings properly in the files of records of the case, admitted in evidence or treated as genuine or admitted to be genuine, by the party against whom the evidence is offered, or proved to be genuine to the satisfaction of the court.

§ 735 ILCS 5/8-1901. Admission of Liability — Effect

The providing of, or payment for, medical, surgical, hospital, or rehabilitation services, facilities,

§ 735 ILCS 5/8-2601.

or equipment by or on behalf of any person, or the offer to provide, or pay for, any one or more of the foregoing, shall not be construed as an admission of any liability by such person or persons. Testimony, writings, records, reports or information with respect to the foregoing shall not be admissible in evidence as an admission of any liability in any action of any kind in any court or before any commission, administrative agency, or other tribunal in this State, except at the instance of the person or persons so making any such provision, payment or offer.

§ 735 ILCS 5/8-2601. Out-of-Court Statement

(a) An out-of-court statement made by a child under the age of 13 describing any act of child abuse or any conduct involving an unlawful sexual act performed in the presence of, with, by, or on the declarant child, or testimony by such of an out-of-court statement made by such child that he or she complained of such acts to another, is admissible in any civil proceeding, if: (1) the court conducts a hearing outside the presence of the jury and finds that the time, content, and circumstances of the statement provide sufficient safeguards of reliability; and (2) the child either: (i) testifies at the proceeding; or (ii) is unavailable as a witness and there is corroborative evidence of the act which is the subject of the statement.

§ 740 ILCS 110/10.

(b) If a statement is admitted pursuant to this Section, the court shall instruct the jury that it is for the jury to determine the weight and credibility to be given to the statement and that, in making its determination, it shall consider the age and maturity of the child, the nature of the statement, the circumstances under which the statement was made, and any other relevant factors.

(c) The proponent of the statement shall give the adverse party reasonable notice of an intention to offer the statement and the particulars of the statement.

§ 740 ILCS 110/10. Disclosure in Civil, Criminal, and Other Proceedings

(a) Except as provided herein, in any civil, criminal, administrative, or legislative proceeding, or in any proceeding preliminary thereto, a recipient, and a therapist on behalf and in the interest of a recipient, has the privilege to refuse to disclose and to prevent the disclosure of the recipient's record or communications.

(1) Records and communications may be disclosed in a civil, criminal or administrative proceeding in which the recipient introduces his mental condition or any aspect of his services received for such condition as an element of his claim or defense, if and only to the extent the court in which the proceedings have been

§ 740 ILCS 110/10.

brought, or, in the case of an administrative proceeding, the court to which an appeal or other action for review of an administrative determination may be taken, finds, after in camera examination of testimony or other evidence, that it is relevant, probative, not unduly prejudicial or inflammatory, and otherwise clearly admissible; that other satisfactory evidence is demonstrably unsatisfactory as evidence of the facts sought to be established by such evidence; and that disclosure is more important to the interests of substantial justice than protection from injury to the therapist-recipient relationship or to the recipient or other whom disclosure is likely to harm. Except in a criminal proceeding in which the recipient, who is accused in that proceeding, raises the defense of insanity, no record or communication between a therapist and a recipient shall be deemed relevant for purposes of this subsection, except the fact of treatment, the cost of services and the ultimate diagnosis unless the party seeking disclosure of the communication clearly establishes in the trial court a compelling need for its production. However, for purposes of this Act, in any action brought or defended under the Illinois Marriage and Dissolution of Marriage Act [750 ILCS 5/101 et seq.], or in any action in which pain and suffering is an element of the claim, mental condition shall not be deemed to

§ 740 ILCS 110/10.

be introduced merely by making such claim and shall be deemed to be introduced only if the recipient or a witness on his behalf first testifies concerning the record or communication.

(2) Records or communications may be disclosed in a civil proceeding after the recipient's death when the recipient's physical or mental condition has been introduced as an element of a claim or defense by any party claiming or defending through or as a beneficiary of the recipient, provided the court finds, after in camera examination of the evidence, that it is relevant, probative, and otherwise clearly admissible; that other satisfactory evidence is not available regarding the facts sought to be established by such evidence; and that disclosure is more important to the interests of substantial justice than protection from any injury which disclosure is likely to cause.

(3) In the event of a claim made or an action filed by a recipient, or, following the recipient's death, by any party claiming as a beneficiary of the recipient for injury caused in the course of providing services to that recipient, the therapist may testify as to pertinent records or communications in any administrative, judicial or discovery proceeding for the purpose of preparing and presenting a defense against the claim or action.

§ 740 ILCS 110/10.

(3.1) A therapist has the right to communicate at any time and in any fashion with his or her own counsel or professional liability insurance carrier, or both, concerning any care or treatment he or she provided, or assisted in providing, to any patient.

(3.2) A therapist has the right to communicate at any time and in any fashion with his or her present or former employer, principal, partner, professional corporation, or professional liability insurance carrier, or counsel for any of those entities, concerning any care or treatment he or she provided, or assisted in providing, to any patient within the scope of his or her employment, affiliation, or other agency with the employer, principal, partner, or professional corporation.

(4) Records and communications made to or by a therapist in the course of examination ordered by a court for good cause shown may, if otherwise relevant and admissible, be disclosed in a civil, criminal, or administrative proceeding in which the recipient is a party or in appropriate pretrial proceedings, provided such court has found that the recipient has been as adequately and as effectively as possible informed before submitting to such examination that such records and communications would not be considered confidential or

§ 740 ILCS 110/10.

privileged. Such records and communications shall be admissible only as to issues involving the recipient's physical or mental condition and only to the extent that these are germane to such proceedings.

(5) Records and communications may be disclosed in a proceeding under the Probate Act of 1975 [755 ILCS 5/1-1 et seq.], to determine a recipient's competency or need for guardianship, provided that the disclosure is made only with respect to that issue.

(6) Records and communications may be disclosed when such are made during treatment which the recipient is ordered to undergo to render him fit to stand trial on a criminal charge, provided that the disclosure is made only with respect to the issue of fitness to stand trial.

(7) Records and communications of the recipient may be disclosed in any civil or administrative proceeding involving the validity of or benefits under a life, accident, health or disability insurance policy or certificate, or Health Care Service Plan Contract, insuring the recipient, but only if and to the extent that the recipient's mental condition, or treatment or services in connection therewith, is a material element of any claim or defense of any party, provided that information sought or disclosed

§ 740 ILCS 110/10.

shall not be redisclosed except in connection with the proceeding in which disclosure is made.

(8) Records or communications may be disclosed when such are relevant to a matter in issue in any action brought under this Act and proceedings preliminary thereto, provided that any information so disclosed shall not be utilized for any other purpose nor be redisclosed except in connection with such action or preliminary proceedings.

(9) Records and communications of the recipient may be disclosed in investigations of and trials for homicide when the disclosure relates directly to the fact or immediate circumstances of the homicide.

(10) Records and communications of a deceased recipient may be disclosed to a coroner conducting a preliminary investigation into the recipient's death under Section 3-3013 of the Counties Code [55 ILCS 5/3-3013]. However, records and communications of the deceased recipient disclosed in an investigation shall be limited solely to the deceased recipient's records and communications relating to the factual circumstances of the incident being investigated in a mental health facility.

(b) Before a disclosure is made under subsection (a), any party to the proceeding or any other interested person may request an in camera review of

§ 740 ILCS 110/10.

the record or communications to be disclosed. The court or agency conducting the proceeding may hold an in camera review on its own motion, except that this provision does not apply to paragraph (3.1) of subsection (a) (regarding consultations between a therapist and his or her own counsel or professional liability insurance carrier) or paragraph (3.2) of subsection (a) (regarding consultations between a therapist and his or her employer, principal, partner, professional corporation, or professional liability insurance carrier, or counsel for any of those entities). When, contrary to the express wish of the recipient, the therapist asserts a privilege on behalf and in the interest of a recipient, the court may require that the therapist, in an in camera hearing, establish that disclosure is not in the best interest of the recipient. The court or agency may prevent disclosure or limit disclosure to the extent that other admissible evidence is sufficient to establish the facts in issue, except that a court may not prevent or limit disclosures between a therapist and his or her own counsel or between a therapist and his or her employer, principal, partner, professional corporation, or professional liability insurance carrier, or counsel for any of those entities. The court or agency may enter such orders as may be necessary in order to protect the confidentiality, privacy, and safety of the recipient or of other persons. Any order to disclose or to not disclose shall be

§ 740 ILCS 110/10.

considered a final order for purposes of appeal and shall be subject to interlocutory appeal.

(c) A recipient records and communications may be disclosed to a duly authorized committee, commission or subcommittee of the General Assembly which possesses subpoena and hearing powers, upon a written request approved by a majority vote of the committee, commission or subcommittee members. The committee, commission or subcommittee may request records only for the purposes of investigating or studying possible violations of recipient rights. The request shall state the purpose for which disclosure is sought.

The facility shall notify the recipient, or his guardian, and therapist in writing of any disclosure request under this subsection within 5 business days after such request. Such notification shall also inform the recipient, or guardian, and therapist of their right to object to the disclosure within 10 business days after receipt of the notification and shall include the name, address and telephone number of the committee, commission or subcommittee member or staff person with whom an objection shall be filed. If no objection has been filed within 15 business days after the request for disclosure, the facility shall disclose the records and communications to the committee, commission or subcommittee. If an objection has been filed within 15 business days after the

§ 740 ILCS 110/10.

request for disclosure, the facility shall disclose the records and communications only after the committee, commission or subcommittee has permitted the recipient, guardian or therapist to present his objection in person before it and has renewed its request for disclosure by a majority vote of its members.

Disclosure under this subsection shall not occur until all personally identifiable data of the recipient and provider are removed from the records and communications. Disclosure under this subsection shall not occur in any public proceeding.

(d) No party to any proceeding described under paragraphs (1), (2), (3), (4), (7), or (8) of subsection (a) of this Section, nor his or her attorney, shall serve a subpoena seeking to obtain access to records or communications under this Act unless the subpoena is accompanied by a written order issued by a judge, authorizing the disclosure of the records or the issuance of the subpoena. No person shall comply with a subpoena for records or communications under this Act, unless the subpoena is accompanied by a written order authorizing the issuance of the subpoena or the disclosure of the records.

This amendatory Act of 1995 applies to causes of action filed on or after its effective date.

§ 810 ILCS 5/2-724.

§ 810 ILCS 5/2-724. Admissibility of Market Quotations

Whenever the prevailing price or value of any goods regularly bought and sold in any established commodity market is in issue, reports in official publications or trade journals or in newspapers or periodicals of general circulation published as the reports of such market shall be admissible in evidence. The circumstances of the preparation of such a report may be shown to affect its weight but not its admissibility.

ILLINOIS SUPREME COURT RULES

Rule 212. Use of Depositions

* * *

(c) Partial Use. If only a part of a deposition is read or used at the trial by a party, any other party may at that time read or use or require him to read any other part of the deposition which ought in fairness to be considered in connection with the part read or used.

* * *

Rule 213. Written Interrogatories to Parties

(a) Directing Interrogatories. A party may direct written interrogatories to any other party. A copy of the interrogatories shall be served on all other parties entitled to notice.

(b) Duty of Attorney. It is the duty of an attorney directing interrogatories to restrict them to the subject matter of the particular case, to avoid undue detail, and to avoid the imposition of any unnecessary burden or expense on the answering party.

(c) Number of Interrogatories. Except as provided in subparagraph (j), a party shall not serve more than 30 interrogatories, including sub-parts,

Rule 213.

on any other party except upon agreement of the parties or leave of court granted upon a showing of good cause. A motion for leave of court to serve more than 30 interrogatories must be in writing and shall set forth the proposed interrogatories and the reasons establishing good cause for their use.

(d) Answers and Objections. Within 28 days after service of the interrogatories upon the party to whom they are directed, the party shall serve a sworn answer or an objection to each interrogatory, with proof of service upon all other parties entitled to notice. Any objection to an answer or to the refusal to answer an interrogatory shall be heard by the court upon prompt notice and motion of the party propounding the interrogatory. The answering party shall set forth in full each interrogatory being answered immediately preceding the answer. Sworn answers to interrogatories directed to a public or private corporation, or a partnership or association shall be made by an officer, partner, or agent, who shall furnish such information as is available to the party.

(e) Option to Produce Documents. When the answer to an interrogatory may be obtained from documents in the possession or control of the party on whom the interrogatory was served, it shall be a sufficient answer to the interrogatory to produce those documents responsive to the interrogatory.

Rule 213.

When a party elects to answer an interrogatory by the production of documents, that production shall comply with the requirements of Rule 214.

(f) Identify and Testimony of Witnesses. Upon written interrogatory, a party must furnish the identity and location of witnesses who will testify at trial, together with the subject of their testimony.

(g) Opinion Witness. An opinion witness is a person who will offer any opinion testimony. Upon written interrogatory, the party must state:

(i) the subject matter on which the opinion witness is expected to testify;

(ii) the conclusions and opinions of the opinion witness and the bases therefor; and

(iii) the qualifications of the opinion witness;

and provide all reports of the opinion witness.

(h) Use of Answers to Interrogatories. Answers to interrogatories may be used in evidence to the same extent as a discovery deposition.

(i) Duty to Supplement. A party has a duty to seasonably supplement or amend any prior answer or response whenever new or additional information subsequently becomes known to that party.

Rule 216.

(j) The Supreme Court, by administrative order, may approve standard forms of interrogatories for different classes of cases.

Rule 216. Admission of Fact or of Genuineness of Documents

(a) Request for Admission of Fact. A party may serve on any other party a written request for the admission by the latter of the truth of any specified relevant fact set forth in the request.

* * *

Rule 220 [Repealed/Reserved]

Former Rule 220, regarding expert witnesses, was repealed June 1, 1995, effective January 1, 1996. See now Rule 213 which refers to opinion witnesses.

[Repealed/Reserved]

Rule 236. Admission of Business Records in Evidence

* * *

(b) Although police accident reports may otherwise be admissible in evidence under the law, subsection (a) of this rule does not allow such writings to be admitted as a record or memorandum made in the regular course of business.

Rule 238. Impeachment of Witnesses; Hostile Witnesses

(a) The credibility of a witness may be attacked by any party, including the party calling him.

Rule 402. Pleas of Guilty or Stipulations Sufficient to Convict

* * *

(f) Plea Discussions, Plea Agreements, Pleas of Guilty Inadmissible Under Certain Circumstances. If a plea discussion does not result in a plea of guilty, or if a plea of guilty is not accepted or is withdrawn, or if judgment on a plea of guilty is reversed on direct or collateral review, neither the plea discussion nor any resulting agreement, plea, or judgment shall be admissible against the defendant in any criminal proceeding.

Rule 433. Impeachment of Witnesses; Hostile Witnesses

The impeachment of witnesses and the examination of hostile witnesses in criminal cases is governed by Rule 238.